JIMMIE
THE KID

JIMMIE THE KID

the Life of Jimmie Rodgers

MIKE PARIS
and
CHRIS COMBER

A DACAPO PAPERBACK

Library of Congress Cataloging in Publication Data

Paris, Mike.
    Jimmie the kid.

    (A Da Capo paperback)
    Reprint of the ed. published by Eddison Press,
London.
    Discography: p.
    Bibliography: p.
    Includes index.
    1. Rodgers, James Charles, 1897-1933. 2. Country
musicians–United States–Biography. I. Comber, Chris,
joint author. II. Title.
    [ML420.R753P4 1981]   784.5′2′00924 [B]   80-29198
    ISBN 0-306-80133-7 (pbk.)

This Da Capo Press paperback edition of
Jimmie the Kid: The Life of Jimmie Rodgers
is an unabridged republication of the
first edition published in London in 1977.
It is reprinted by arrangement with
Eddison Press Ltd.

Quotations from Jimmie Rodgers' songs are reproduced
by kind permission of Southern Music Publishing Co.
Ltd. London who have available a fine book of over
twenty of Jimmie Rodgers' most famous songs
entitled "JIMMIE RODGERS" – Country Song Hall
of Fame No. 8 compiled by Allan Dann and John
Underwood and on sale at most music stockists.

Published by Da Capo Press, Inc.
A Subsidiary of Plenum Publishing Corporation
227 West 17th Street, New York, N.Y. 10011

Contents

Introduction

It is now over forty years since Jimmie Rodgers died; yet for a singer of country music, the years since 1933 have seen an unprecedented amount of literature published about his life and musical career. But with the exception of the biography written by his wife Carrie, there has never been a full-length study of Rodgers — and even that book is tantalisingly brief regarding his musical career. Certainly the continuing popularity of 'The Singing Brakeman' and his enormous influence on country music justifies a new examination of his life and work. Here we have attempted to present a detailed biography and an analysis of his music; thus there may be some material that is not common knowledge amongst aficionados, but it has not been our intention to repeat gossip or unsubstantiated rumour. It has not been easy to determine the truth behind many incidents in his life, and it seems likely that there is much about Jimmie Rodgers' career that is lost forever.

Rodgers was certainly an enigmatic and paradoxical figure. In his life-style there is much that is reminiscent of the mediaeval minstrel, the wandering balladeer. Yet he was the first star entertainer in the field of country music. In many ways, he was what might be termed a popular entertainer; but his style and repertoire were deeply rooted in the traditions of the rural South. A dedicated family man, Jimmie was also a 'rounder' and a 'hell-raiser'. He achieved great success in music, but only after failing at his chosen profession and first love, the railroad. Jimmie Rodgers was a man of great courage and determination. He was also an opportunist: a man both humble and arrogant. His musical influence on the style of country music was enormous, yet who today records a blue yodel? It even seems possible that he was an early victim of the exploitation which today is so common amongst popular entertainers. Even now, only forty years since his death, it is increasingly difficult to separate the man from the legend. It has been our intention to shed a little more light on one of the most influential artists in country music; if we have not succeeded, then perhaps we may at least have paved the way for later researchers.

This book has been researched and written over a period of three years. During that time we have received considerable help and support from fellow researchers and collectors. Particularly, we owe a great deal to Nolan Porterfield in Missouri; Jake Smith in Mississippi; Anita Rodgers Court in Texas; Dwight Butcher in California; Dave Samuelson in Indiana, and Frank Mare in New York. In London we have incurred many debts. Particularly our thanks go to George Tye, Tony Russell, John Stoten, Brian Rust and Richard Weize; and to the many collectors and researchers who have delved into the early history of the music and made this present work possible.

Mike Paris and Chris Comber
London, 1975

PICTURE CREDITS

Photographs are reproduced by kind permission of their owners or copyright-holders, as follows:

David Evans   38
Jim Evans   12, 13, 15, 17, 41, 74, 77, 82T, 89B, 112, 113, 130, 154L, 155TL, 155B, 159T, 160, 161 (all), 166
Carl Fleischhauer   127, 170
John Edwards Memorial Foundation   94L, 94R, 117
Meridian *Star*   154R, 155TR, 156B, 157T, 158
Old Time Music Library   49, 60, 75, 79, 97
Sylvia Pitcher   61L, 61R
Mrs. Lillian Rush   53R
Dave Samuelson   40, 43
George W Tye   153B

All other illustrations are from the authors' collection.

1 / Rough and Rowdy Ways

For years and years I've rambled;
Drank my wine and gambled.

(My Rough and Rowdy Ways)

Mississippi has been a state of the Union since 1817, and even though it is one of America's smaller states, its population and area are entirely disproportionate: barely two million on more than 47,000 square miles. The state is bounded on the east by Alabama, by Tennessee on the north, and on the west by Louisiana and Arkansas, where the state line follows the course of the great Mississippi River. Mississippi, both in location and culture, is firmly wedded to the Deep South.

Mississippi is cotton country — flat, rich and easy to work. And because, in the days before mechanisation, the cotton crop required cheap and plentiful labour, Mississippi was slave country. In the main cotton counties, such as Yazoo and Sunflower, the majority of the population were (and still are) black. Even in other areas blacks heavily outnumber the white population. During the Civil War, white Mississippians marched proudly, but blindly, against the Union to preserve their slave-based economy, and the state was subsequently ravaged by the victorious Yankees. Now, unable to subjugate the black population by legal means, the extremists turned their backs on the law and thus were born the notorious klaverns of the Ku Klux Klan. Beating, lynching and other terrorist activities were employed to deter any black foolish enough to insist upon the equality to which the Fifth Amendment entitled him. The theoretical freedom given to the black man by the Civil War had little practical application in the South, for freed from actual bondage they were still enslaved by the feudal sharecropping system of farming. Yet if life was hard for the black it was no less hard for the poor Southern white. The white sharecropper was also imprisoned by this archaic system, where crop failure, drought or flood brought the very real prospect of starvation for the farmer and his family. Throughout the Southern states there is a lack of industry which could offer alternative occupations; and Mississippi suffers from this more, perhaps, than most states. Except for lumbering in the north and river work along the banks of the Mississippi, the state has little to offer. There are few cities and only a handful of larger towns. Jackson — the state's capital — has even today a population of only 150,000. Vicksburg, Hattiesburg, Biloxi, Gulfport and Natchez are important centres: but their importance rests as much upon their being railroad junctions as upon their light and limited industry. The poverty, the unhealthy climate and the extreme racial bigotry make Mississippi one of the most backward rural areas in the whole United States.

But if Mississippi was poor economically, it was rich in its traditional music. Much has been written on the importance of the state in the development of Afro-American music — and a good case could be made for the argument that the blues (in their first recognisable form) even originated from the Mississippi Delta counties.[1] Certainly, the singers and music of rural Mississippi wielded an enormous influence on the whole development of black American music. It seems fitting, then, that the white singer who was to be the watershed in the development of white rural music (variously known as 'hillbilly' or 'country music') should also be a native of that state.

Last Gap is a farming community near the city of Meridian and here Aaron W. Rodgers and his wife Eliza Bozeman were living when their third son, James Charles Rodgers, was born on 8 September 1897. The Rodgerses were of Scots—Irish origin and may have descended from the trappers and hunters who had settled the Mississippi Valley in the early 19th century. The family name appears to have always been spelled Rogers but Aaron added the 'd' and he (and later Jimmie) was insistent upon the new spelling. At the time of Jimmie's birth, Aaron Rodgers was working for the Gulf, Mobile and Ohio Railroad as an extra-gang foreman. The extra-gang were repair men who were sent to any section of the line which was in need of urgent attention. This meant that Aaron was frequently away from home, often for days at a time. Shortly after Jimmie's birth, Aaron decided to leave the railroad and try his hand at farming. The family moved to Pine Springs, a small town north of Meridian and the home area of the Bozeman family. Aaron rented land and a comfortable old farm house just outside the town.

In 1901, when Jimmie was four years old, his mother died of tuberculosis. For a short period he was sent to live with his father's relatives in Scooba, Alabama, but soon returned to his father. Two years later, Aaron married Ida Love Smith, a young widow of Pine Springs. Ida, by her first marriage, already had a four year old son, Jake. (Today Jake Smith lives in Meridian, and it is to him that we are indebted for much of the information in this chapter.) However, by 1904, Aaron Rodgers realised that to support his family he would have to return to railroad work. He gave up his land and moved to Meridian, finding work on the New Orleans and North Eastern Line.

Meridian, one of the more important cities in Mississippi, lies 150 miles east of Vicksburg in Lauderdale County and close to the Alabama line. A modest industrial and lumbering centre, its chief importance is as a railroad junction. During the Civil War, Meridian had been almost totally destroyed by Sherman's troops for harbouring Confederate guerillas. Thus, when the Rodgerses arrived, Meridian was a comparatively newly built city. Although Jimmie Rodgers was to be closely associated with Meridian, this first visit was for only one year. Aaron was offered the job of manager of a large alfalfa farm in Artesia, in Lowndes County. The farm was owned by Miss Estelle Smith, a distant relative of his second wife. It was in Artesia that Jimmie, now aged eight, and young Jake Smith began to attend a local public school. The building was several miles from the Rodgers home and the boys made the daily journey on a mule named Association. During this period Jimmie was often ill with one complaint following another. It seemed as if he had inherited his mother's fragile health. In 1906 the family again moved, to West Point in Clay County. Their stay in West Point was brief and they soon returned to Meridian where Aaron again took up railroad work. He acquired a large timbered house about a mile outside the city limits, for the Rodgers family was growing — another child, a daughter named Lottie Mae, had been born to Aaron and Ida in the early part of 1906.

Aaron was often away from home at this time and, whenever they could, young Jimmie and Jake would skip school and in Jake's words 'do a little business'.[2] Their business was selling jugs of molasses at the side of the main road into the city. The price was five dollars a jug, but the boys were never known to refuse a reasonable offer. However, in 1911, Ida Smith Rodgers died. Jake and his sister Lottie were sent to live with their mother's relatives, and Jake recalled that after this his close association with Jimmie ended.

Aaron kept on the large house and continued with railroad work, and Jimmie was often on his own for long periods. His oldest brother Talmadge was now working for the Meridian Police Office and Walter for the railroad. Sometimes Aaron managed to take Jimmie with him on his trips up the line but more often than not Jimmie was left on his own. Later, Carrie Rodgers, in her biography of her husband, has recalled the story of Jimmie begging for milk from local cafes to go with the corn flakes he had 'acquired'.[3] The story has a certain folksy quality but it

Above, *the school Rodgers attended in Meridian.* Right, *his home during his railroading days.*

seems unlikely that the Rodgerses were ever in such a desperate financial situation.

Understandably, the many moves the family made during Jimmie's formative years would have left some mark on his personality. This, and the lack of stable family relationships, probably left Jimmie with a deep restlessness and a keen sense of insecurity; and these factors may help to explain his forceful, brash personality, and the desperate, almost fanatical, attempts he made in later years to keep his own family together in the face of personal and financial difficulties. But whatever the psychological influences of his early years, about the year 1911 he came into contact with what Jerry Silverman has called the symbol of his life — the railroad train.[4] While waiting for his father to return from jobs up the line, Jimmie took to hanging round the Meridian freight yards, and here, as Silverman has noted in somewhat folksy prose,

> He absorbed the lingo, the yarns, and the songs of the railroaders, those wonderful, wandering men who had been everywhere, seen and done everything, and had come back to tell about it.[5]

Much has been written about the significance and symbolism of the train in American folk literature. Alan Lomax has even suggested that the

railroad was the inspiration of the 'greatest body of good American music'.[6] Certainly there is no sphere of music in which railroad themes are not recurrrent: pop, jazz, folk, blues and hillbilly, all have their share of railroad songs and instrumentals. And certainly, the growth of the American railroad system was spectacular enough to capture anyone's imagination. From its timid beginnings in the 1820s, 30,000 miles of track were in use by 1860. But in the decade from 1880, over 70,000 miles of line were added. At their peak, the railroad companies operated over 254,000 miles of gleaming steel track, and added such names as the Lackawanna, Rock Island, Southern Pacific and Soo Line to folk literature.

It is possible that the railroad train became so easily a folk symbol because it represented so much to so many different sections of the population. To most people, though, it was perhaps a symbol of freedom: a concrete expression of the tremendous restlessness so much a part of the American character: a means of 'movin' on' and seeking better times and places. For the Southern black and poor white it symbolised escape from a repressed and depressed South. For the merchant, the manufacturer, and the farmer, it meant a new prosperity: a safe and economical means of transporting goods and produce. For the lonely, a smoking locomotive pounding across the prairie or through the swampland, sending its lonesome whistle echoing into the night, personified their loneliness. And the sheer size and power of a locomotive captured the imagination of men and boys throughout the continent. Little wonder, then, that a young and lonely boy like Jimmie Rodgers should become fascinated by the locomotives; by the exclusive brotherhood of tough railroaders in faded, oil-stained denim and 'thousand mile' shirts, and by the romantic world of the eight-wheel flyers, the Fireball Mail and the Cannonball.

Through his contacts with Meridian's railroaders, Jimmie soon knew as much about signals, fast freights, and passenger expresses as any other railroader. At the end of his 14th year, the little contact he had had with formal education ended and, together with his friend Mike Murphy, he began as a water boy in the freight yards. Water boys carried water to the workmen and received tips from them for their trouble. Carrie Rodgers claimed that Jimmie and Mike received around 50 cents a day for this.[7] Because of the extreme racial segregation in Mississippi, it would seem to be unusual for a white boy to carry water to black workers, the job usually being reserved for young blacks. Unusual but not unique: although it is to be assumed that the blacks would be fairly respectful to the young white boys. But here, from these black railroad workers, Jimmie Rodgers began to develop a serious interest in music.

While still very young Jimmie had developed an intense interest in show business. When living with his aunt in Scooba, he had borrowed his sister-in-law's bed sheets to make his own tent show; and later in Meridian, had used his father's credit account to buy a tent to set up a 'real' show. According to his aunt, Jimmie had always been able to put over a song, and at the age of 12 had won a talent show in a Meridian theatre with his singing of *Bill Bailey* and *Steamboat Bill.*[8] With his background of loneliness and neglect (however unintentional), it is easy to see how performing, singing or some other aspect of show-life would appeal to Jimmie — an instant means of acquiring friends and popularity. But now, in the Meridian yards, his musical education began in earnest. At this time, as Rodgers authority Nolan Porterfield has pointed out,

> Jimmie learned two essentials which were to mark the course of his life: (i) the human condition, at its best, is a tough proposition, and (ii) music helps to lighten the load.[9]

In the yards, from the blacks (and probably the white workers as well), Jimmie began to learn the rudiments of the guitar and banjo and probably other stringed instruments.

Just how influential this early tuition was in the development of Jimmie's playing is difficult to determine, for it was to be 16 years before he first recorded his music. In the past, some writers have given the impression that this early experience was tremendously important: that after this Jimmie Rodgers emerged as a fully-fledged blues singer and instrumentalist. But this is most unlikely. After all, Rodgers had no desire at this time other than to amuse himself; and had only the incentive to

Meridian in the early '50s.

learn that anyone has who has a new interest to be enjoyed at leisure. Furthermore, the blues form itself was still in a state of development. In fact, it now seems likely that the blues did not reach its early recognisable form until shortly before it was first commercially recorded, in the early 1920s. Most probably, then, Jimmie merely picked up the rudiments of the guitar and banjo, and likely concentrated more on the banjo. That Rodgers considered himself primarily a banjo player until the mid-'20s (and perhaps even as late as his early recordings) seems to be borne out by three pieces of evidence: his wife's frequent references to his dissatisfaction with his guitar playing; comments made by Goebel Reeves, the hobo songster who met Jimmie in 1923, and claimed that Jimmie played better banjo than guitar; and when Rodgers finally formed his band in 1927, he almost certainly played tenor banjo. It is also significant that when Rodgers and the band split, Jimmie's place was taken by a tenor banjo player.

Nevertheless, in the Meridian freight yards Jimmie must certainly have learned the worksongs and chants of the black workers (both elements that contributed to the blues form). From then on, it appears that Jimmie always carried round a stringed instrument — banjo, guitar, mandolin or ukulele. During his work breaks or lunch hours Jimmie would entertain his fellow workers. In the evenings he would join fellow part-time musicians round Meridian, and often sat in with black pickers on Tenth Street. One accepts that music breaks down barriers of race and colour, but in Mississippi, by the standards of the early 1900s (and even today), Rodgers' frequent contacts with blacks would appear fairly unusual. Mississippi had, and still has, some of the most extreme racialist elements in the entire South. Thus, although Rodgers was not unique in his contacts, they serve as useful pointers that in his character there was no room for the racial bigotry so common in that place and time. It is also interesting to note that, unlike many of his fellow recording artists at that time, Jimmie did not have a strong musical background. His grandfather Zachary did play the fiddle, and passed the instrument on to Jimmie's brother Talmadge who played occasionally. But neither Aaron nor his two wives played or sang.

Throughout that summer and autumn of 1911, Jimmie and his friend carried water, and then Jimmie's father arranged for him to be taken on as his assistant. But Jimmie wanted to be a 'real' railroader and in 1913 managed to become a brakeman on the line's freight trains. Jimmie's brother Walter, a railroad employee of some years' standing, then got him on the passenger runs from Meridian to New Orleans on the Gulf-Mobile Line. From then, until tuberculosis made it impossible for him to continue, Jimmie worked at what he knew and liked best – railroading. During this period he filled every job, from call-boy to flagman, baggage master to brakeman.

Photographs of Jimmie in his late teens and early twenties show a good-looking, somewhat chubby-faced, neatly dressed young man, brown-haired and brown-eyed. According to his wife, Jimmie was always meticulous in his dress, even when he was broke and his clothes threadbare. His neat appearance pleased the railroad inspectors and when special trains were run, it was often Jimmie who was chosen as flagman. About this time he also picked up his lifelong habit of carrying scent.

> He always loved perfume and nearly always carried a tiny flask in his vest pocket; not caring in the least if folks wanted to consider it 'funny'. In the beginning I think he turned to it as a change from the smell of the railroad yards; oiled waste and gas-laden coal smoke. Later, perfume became for him a welcome relief from iodoform and antiseptics.[10]

Like any young man, Jimmie was fond of girls and enjoyed a good time, and while he was in regular employment he could well afford to enjoy himself. During the years immediately preceding World War I there was no lack of work. It was about this time that Jimmie Rodgers married for the first time.

The full circumstances of Jimmie's first marriage will probably never be known. Once Jimmie had achieved his success, his immediate family and close friends were reluctant even to reveal that he was married before he

Jimmie at 19.

met Carrie Williamson, as it was felt that this knowledge might harm his image. After so many years, the facts have been forgotten and only bare statements in official records bear witness to the event. It is sufficient for the purpose of this book to relate the details briefly as the affair had little lasting effect on the remainder of his life. Around 1916, Jimmie met and married a local Meridian girl. A child, a daughter, was born to the couple. However, the marriage lasted for only two years and ended in annulment. But from then until his death, Jimmie made financial provision for the child. Both his first wife and daughter are now dead.

* * *

On 17 April 1917 President Woodrow Wilson led America into World War I. By October 1918 America had an army of well over one million men in France. This enormous mobilisation of men and military equipment meant that the railroads were kept constantly at maximum operation. The government took over the running of the privately owned companies and exempted railroad men from the draft. Jimmie and his companions, however, were called upon to work longer shifts in all weathers. One particular friend, a Meridian boy named Sammy Williams, had volunteered and was killed in France. The news of his death prompted Jimmie to write a musical tribute, *The Soldier's Sweetheart* — generally accepted as his first composition. However, the song is based upon a much older traditional ballad, *Once I Had a Sweetheart*. But even so, nine years later the song was still used for his first recording. According to Carrie Rodgers, Jimmie's friends liked *Sweetheart* and Jimmie was often requested to play it. Although this could be termed a country song, most of Jimmie's repertoire at this time seems to have been composed of the sentimental ballads and popular songs then in vogue: *Sweet Adeline* and similar songs. Apart from his sessions with Meridian's black musicians, most of his playing, according to Claudia Rigby-Vick, was in the parlours of respectable Meridian homes for well-chaperoned young ladies.[11] In 1919, in one such parlour, he was to meet his second wife, Carrie Cecil Williamson.

It should be said here that the main account of Jimmie's life from 1919 onwards is Carrie Rodgers' biography *My Husband Jimmie Rodgers*. This is a sentimental and romanticised account of his life, which nevertheless contains much useful information on the years preceding his rise to fame. The book is rarely specific as to dates, people or important events, and frequently gives conflicting accounts of controversial points in Jimmie's career. Where these occur, we have noted them in the text. It is the only source for details of his personal life and we have been forced to rely upon it to a considerable extent. Unfortunately, it completely omits anything which might be thought to have been harmful to Jimmie's image, even though it was written two years after his death. Thus, although interesting, the book must be read with caution.

The Reverend Jesse T. and Kizzie Ann Williamson orginally came from Harperville, Scott County, in central Mississippi, where the Reverend had a farm. The Williamsons' children had all been born in Harpersville for the family did not move to Meridian until around the year 1915. Carrie Cecil was the second youngest in a family of nine children, six girls and three boys. At the time of her first meeting with Jimmie Rodgers she was nearly 14 years old and still attending school in Meridian. The Williamsons were highly respectable but almost certainly poor. However, they frequently entertained at their home.

One evening in the summer of 1919, a mutual girl friend introduced Jimmie Rodgers to the family. Carrie has described her first embarrassing meeting with the young brakeman, for the visitors arrived unexpectedly while Carrie was 'ploughing her face with cold cream'.

> I had just finished the kitchen work and was hurrying to get to my lessons. None of us expected callers that night. Before I realised it, our mutual friend and a strange young man were staring at me — laughing and teasing.[12]

However, the family gathered in the parlour and Carrie, now suitably dressed for company, joined them around the piano, sneaking sly looks at the young railroadman.

The next meeting was no less embarrassing for Carrie, for Jimmie arrived while she was wearing old clothes and 'wearing in' her brother's new shoes. But Jimmie had come fully equipped for courting and had brought his banjo and a large box of candy. He soon became a frequent visitor at the Williamson home. He enjoyed the easy-going, relaxed family atmosphere and liked looking through the many songbooks in the house. As with most families in the age before mass entertainment, the Williamsons made their own music. Reverend Jesse and his wife had recorded several cylinder records in the years before coming to Meridian (although, as far as we know, these have never been traced). All six daughters played musical instruments, and two were particularly talented. The eldest, Annie, was a qualified piano teacher, and Elsie (later Elsie McWilliams) was eventually to notate and co-write many of Jimmie's songs, as well as being a composer and songwriter in her own right. However, Elsie was not to meet Jimmie until after his marriage to her sister, for she had married in 1917 and lived for the next three years in Washington.

Throughout the summer and autumn, Jimmie and Carrie saw each other frequently, but even at this time Jimmie's life style was causing her some concern. She recalled that after a trip (Jimmie was now working for the New Orleans and North Eastern Line, which he had joined in 1918), he

Over page, *Jimmie aged 20.*

would be off for a good time, singing and playing with his friends. Nevertheless, she had almost made her mind to marry the brakeman, who frequently proposed.

In the autumn of 1919, a serious influenza epidemic raged through the South. Both Carrie's sister and mother were among the victims. Mrs Williamson became so ill that it was thought she might die, for she was unable to eat or sleep. One evening Jimmie and his friends arrived at the house and despite Carrie's protests, began to play a little music in the parlour. Carrie at first thought that the noise would disturb her mother, but found that the soft music had lulled her mother into a deep sleep -- the first proper rest she had had for some time. The next day Mrs Williamson began to recover, and Carrie became convinced that Jimmie had saved her mother's life.

In the spring of 1920, Jimmie caught a heavy cold. He paid little attention to it but eventually it turned to pneumonia. Carrie had not seen him for several weeks and so, suitably chaperoned by a girlfriend, she called at his home. Jimmie had almost recovered from his illness and while the girlfriend was out of the room, he once again proposed. This time Carrie accepted. As she later wrote, 'I'd decided that having Jimmie was better than school'.[13] The next day Jimmie bought a $12 ring and a special licence. At 12.30 pm on 7 April 1920 James Charles Rodgers and Carrie Cecil Williamson were married by the Reverend J. L. Sells in Meridian. On a free railroad company pass the couple travelled to New Orleans for a three-day honeymoon.

2 / A Brakeman's Blues

I went to the depot and I looked up on the board,
It said good times here, but better down the road.

(The Brakeman's Blues)

It would seem that Jimmie's marriage was very much against the wishes of Carrie's parents; possibly because of Carrie's age (after all, she was only 14 years old), but more likely because of the considerable differences in their families and background. Rodgers, a reckless, footloose railroader, had never settled anywhere very long, and railroading was not the most secure of occupations. His first marriage had resulted in divorce, and he was an associate of Meridian's less-than-respectable musicians' circle. It even seems possible that his tuberculosis may have been diagnosed as early as 1918. If this were so, then it would certainly have been another objection raised by Carrie's parents. The Williamsons, however, were an established and highly respectable family: Carrie's brother Nate even became a state senator in later years. Her background was strict and religious and it was presumably expected that she would remain at school for some years, and perhaps eventually become a teacher like her sister Annie. Just how much her parents objected to the marriage is not known, but it seems likely that they were presented with a *fait accompli* by Jimmie and Carrie getting married first and telling her parents afterwards. This seems to be borne out by the fact that they were married by Rev. Sells, when one would have expected Carrie's father to officiate. And by her own words,

> After that runaway three-day honeymoon of ours, when Jimmie Rodgers, railroader, and his schoolgirl bride went back — not ashamed or regretful, but a bit uncertain, maybe — home to Meridian for the parental blessing.'[1]

But whatever the Williamsons' initial reactions, they must have accepted the fact for they were frequently to help the young couple in the years ahead.

Through his childhood experiences, Jimmie Rodgers was almost certainly addicted to a restless, wandering life style. From the start of his working life this had been reinforced by riding trains all over the South, never stopping long in any one place. He had grown accustomed to 'moving on', and it seems that even marriage and children made little difference. But the railroad boom caused by the war was ending, and many of Rodgers' future travels were caused by economic necessity. The Transportation Acts of 1920 denationalised the railroads and put the companies back into the hands of private enterprise. To ensure that they once again ran as profitable concerns, a certain pruning of staff was necessary and many employees now found themselves without jobs or temporarily laid off. Jimmie Rodgers was no exception, and the next few years of his life were to be difficult ones. As Carrie Rodgers recalled, jobs became scarcer and when Jimmie was wanted it often meant moving to another town. Of this period she wrote:

> As for me . . . I was thankful whenever he had a call, a job; even when it meant that gay 'Throw your things together, kid. We're leaving here for there.' Very soon I learned to keep my things thrown together.[2]

Shortly after their marriage, Jimmie worked for a short period in New Orleans. Here, Jimmie and Carrie lived in a cheap railroad boarding house at a lonely junction just outside the city. But despite the considerable differences in their backgrounds, the couple appears to have been happy. Carrie wanted to settle somewhere and put down roots. Jimmie would probably have fallen in with her wishes (at least for a while) had his job not necessitated considerable mobility. At first, it seems as if Jimmie rarely worried about the future or about financial security. Carrie economised as much as possible and usually managed to save half of whatever Jimmie gave her. But towards the end of the year Jimmie was laid off. Carrie was expecting their first child and the future looked bleak. Soon after Christmas Jimmie was taken back as a brakeman. On his first run, on 30 January 1921, a message reached him that Carrie had given birth to a daughter. Jimmie found a substitute to relieve him and took the first train back to Meridian. The child was christened Carrie Anita, after her mother and Anita Stewart, a then popular actress whom both Jimmie and Carrie greatly admired. As railroading was proving such a precarious occupation, Jimmie decided to try another form of work — something which might provide greater security for his family.

Towards the end of 1921 Jimmie even tried his hand at farming. He took land near the town of Purvis, but found that farming was an even tougher proposition than railroading. After giving up the farm he crossed the state line into Alabama, to the town of Geiger where his father was then living. Here Jimmie drove trucks for a dollar a day. However, the driving did not last long, and Jimmie was soon back in his native Mississippi working whenever he could on the railroad. In June 1923 his second daughter, June Rebecca, was born. Unlike Anita, who was blond and blue-eyed, June was olive-skinned and dark-eyed like her father. But the birth of June marked the beginning of a period of hardship and personal tragedy for the Rodgerses.

In the autumn Anita nearly died of diptheria. Shortly after this, Jimmie found himself once again temporarily laid off. Christmas found him job-hunting in New Orleans. However, the railroads had all the men they

Left, *Goebel Reeves, 'The Texas Drifter'*, c. *1934*. Above, *Jimmie, Carrie and Anita outside their Meridian home*, c. *1923*.

needed and Jimmie had little luck. He spent a lot of his time hanging round Canal Street, meeting and talking with musicians; and here he met Goebel Reeves, a singer and guitarist who later recorded as the 'Texas Drifter'. Goebel Leon Reeves was a born wanderer. He had enlisted as a private in the army in 1917 and after his discharge had taken to the hobo life. His travels had taken him all over America, Europe and even Japan. A fine singer and a most distinctive yodeller, he recorded many sides for Okeh, Brunswick, Gennett, ARC and Decca between 1929 and 1934 and in 1938-9 recorded some 50 transcriptions for the MacGregor Company in California.

However, Jimmie was depressed over his failure to find work in the city. Thinking that even if he was broke, Christmas would be a more cheerful affair if he was at home with his family, he pawned his banjo for the train fare and headed back to Meridian. But at home even worse news awaited him. His second daughter, June, was dead. The Rodgerses were in such desperate financial difficulties that they could not even pay for the funeral and relatives had to help with the expenses.

For Jimmie's life in the period 1924-7, the researcher is faced with many problems. The only full account of these years is the book by his wife. However, for these years Carrie mentions no specific dates between 1924 and January 1927. A reconstruction of the events she mentions and tentative dates would run as follows. In early 1924, Jimmie found work in Utah and Colorado. He returned home a few months later and suffered what Carrie calls his first haemorrhage. After his recovery in the summer, he joined a medicine show travelling through the mountains of Kentucky and Tennessee. Eventually he formed his own show but this was destroyed by freak winds. He returned to Meridian, rejoined Carrie and together they went to Florida, where he worked for almost a year for the Florida and East Coast line. According to Carrie's chronology this would be about early 1926. Finding that the damp Florida climate did not suit his health, they left for Arizona where Jimmie found a job on the Southern Pacific line. At the end of the year he returned to Mississippi via Texas. In early 1927 he went to Asheville, North Carolina, and in May of that year formed the Jimmie Rodgers Entertainers. However, in the light of Nolan Porterfield's research, this chronological outline, and even the events themselves, is highly suspect. The matter is further confused by the reminiscences of Albert Fullam, a locomotive engineer who worked with Jimmie in his railroad days.

Porterfield discovered amongst the Rodgers papers in the possession of Anita Court, Jimmie's daughter, a letter of recommendation from the New Orleans and North Eastern Railroad Company, written when Jimmie terminated his employment with the line. The letter reads as follows:

Hattiesburg, Miss. Jan'y 17th 1925.

TO WHOM IT MAY CONCERN,

J. C. Rodgers has been employed by NO&NER since January 9, 1918 on account ill health is going west and seaking [sic] such employment that he can get any favors shown him will be appreciated

Yours Truly,

/S/   A. M. Tipton

Train Masiter [sic] [3]

Railroading at Jimmie's level was never a very secure occupation, and given the economic conditions in the South fifty years ago, it is easy to see that there would be many layoffs and enforced vacations. However, this letter is a far more reliable source than Mrs Rodgers' book for dating Jimmie's movements; and it establishes, beyond doubt, that Jimmie did not leave Mississippi looking for railroad work until after the Christmas of 1924. However, the document may solve some problems, but it makes the period after 1925 far harder to date. It is now our invidious task to attempt a new, and speculative, chronology for this part of Jimmie's life (and here we must acknowledge a considerable debt to the research of Nolan Porterfield).

Carrie Rodgers has stated that in 1924 Jimmie suffered his first severe lung haemorrhage; and there seems no reason to doubt that it was, in fact, the early part of that year. During this period in the South tuberculosis was amongst the most virulent and widely-spread diseases. It is often inherited, or can be contacted from other sufferers, and usually remains undetected until it is too far advanced for a cure to be effected. Possibly

Jimmie inherited this from his mother and the disease had been exacerbated by his railroad work and poor living conditions; finally breaking out after the severe winter of '23. There is, of course, the possibility that Rodgers contracted the disease from the blacks he was associated with. Tuberculosis was, at that time, endemic amongst the black population of the South — easily brought on by poor living conditions and easily spread by the overcrowded living accommodation in Southern cities and rural towns. That it was a common fact of life is testified to by the large number of blues which refer to it. But whatever the cause of the disease, tuberculosis was to be a major influence on Jimmie's way of life from now on.

For three months Jimmie lay in a charity hospital outside Meridian, while Carrie travelled the four miles every day to visit him. Sometimes she had the bus fare, sometimes she walked. When Jimmie left the hospital in the spring, the doctors advised him that he desperately needed a warm, dry climate, and should avoid all physical exertion. Railroading was just about the worst possible occupation for a man in his condition for it was exhausting and meant exposure to all weathers. But Jimmie, with characteristic stubbornness, had little intention of following his doctor's orders. He was a railroadman and he was going to work the trains, as soon as he was strong enough. After all, he had a wife and daughter to support and was untrained for any other job. In the summer Jimmie felt much stronger and was sure he could work again. Railroading was still out of the question, but his other great interest was music, and perhaps music could help him solve his immediate problems.

Throughout the early years of his marriage Jimmie had never lost his interest in music; and probably, like so many others facing hard times, music helped him to cope with his problems. Carrie Rodgers has recalled how, during the early years, he would often wake her in the middle of the night with an idea for a new song, a title, or perhaps just an odd line. Eventually, she developed the habit of keeping a pencil and paper beside the bed so that these ideas could be noted down. One of the few luxuries that the Rodgerses indulged in at this time was gramophone records — but Jimmie was a critical listener.

> Working tirelessly towards the betterment of his own brand of music making, he would play those records over and over. Then he would say, displeased: 'That guy ought to tone down that banjo. Got a pretty good voice, but shucks, what's the use of having a good voice if it's all the time drowned out?' Other times he'd say, 'Doggone! That guy's a humdinger on the mandolin, but his singing is a pain in the neck.'[4]

Of course, one would dearly like to know what records Jimmie bought, but Carrie, as usual, gives no clue at all. However, Jimmie, in addition to his semi-professional and amateur performances, had had one brief spell as a full-time musician. During one lay-off from the NO&NER, in the summer of 1923, he had joined a travelling tent show, Billy Terrell's Comedians. Terrell himself has told the story of Rodgers' first professional engagement.

Billy Terrell and his wife Bonnie were veterans of the theatrical world. During the early '20s, they operated one of the country's biggest tent shows, often employing as many as forty-five performers. Their usual operating area was Tennessee, the Carolinas, Virginia and Kentucky, and westwards into Arkansas, Missouri and Texas. In the summer of 1923 they were in Meridian, Mississippi for a two-week engagement.

Jimmie saw the show, and with nothing to lose, asked Terrell if he could 'try out to see if he could make it in show business'.[5] Terrell gave him the chance, but refused to let him go on in Meridian.

> No, I told him. 'Don't ever break in your home town, for you are usually razzed and criticised.' Jimmie was such a pleasant fellow, and after he told me he was a blue yodeller, something I had never heard of, I listened to him one afternoon at my hotel room; after he had finished I said, 'You certainly have something that is different, and we jump to Hattiesburg, and if you will go you can get a try out.'[6]

The show moved to Hattiesburg and opened on a Monday night.

> The tent was packed . . . and I gave him a real build-up, out came Jimmie, with that big smile on his face, he walked to the centre of the stage and started whipping that old guitar − then he pulled his train whistle and he had them in his hand.
>
> Jimmie did two numbers and took three big encores . . . From that time on Jimmie was a big favourite with the show as well as the audiences, in the cities we played . . . but after eight weeks he began to get homesick for his wife and daughter . . . and said that old railroad was calling him back. I honestly believe that our show 'Billy Terrell's Comedians' was Jimmie's first trouping.[7]

Back in Meridian, Jimmie formed a small group that included Slim Rozell (whom Rodgers had met while with Terrell) on trombone and Elsie McWilliams (his sister-in-law) on piano. Rodgers presumably played banjo and some guitar. The group, according to Elsie, had no professional aspirations but were content to play for local parties, picnics and fairs in a purely amateur capacity.[8] Now, unable to work on the railroads, and completely untrained for any other occupation, Jimmie Rodgers turned to music in order to support his family.

Medicine shows, with their glib quack doctors selling patent, and usually worthless, cure-alls, were a common sight throughout the rural areas at this time. These shows apparently became popular after the Civil War and continued well into the late '30s. Almost every doctor featured entertainers − comedians or singers, often in blackface. The entertainers' function was to attract a crowd and put the audience into a good humour before the doctor began his sales patter. As Bill Malone has pointed out, these shows served two useful functions in the development of country

Jimmie touring with a medicine show.

music. First, they introduced new songs and musical styles to the rural areas — an important means of dissemination in the days before records and radio. And secondly, they provided a commercial outlet for country and blues musicians.[9] Clarence Ashley, John Carson, Uncle Dave Macon, Dock Walsh and Bradley Kincaid, amongst others, all gained their initial professional experience in such shows; as well as a whole host of fine blues musicians such as Furry Lewis, Jim Jackson and Gus Cannon. Now, Jimmie Rodgers blacked his face, took up his banjo, and joined one such show travelling through the mountains of Kentucky and Tennessee. On one show he worked with the influential blues singer Frank Stokes. Stokes, a native of Memphis, was long associated with Dan Sane, another fine guitarist, with whom he recorded for Paramount as the Beale Street Sheiks.

While working blackface, Rodgers developed an uncanny knack of imitating blacks. The Kentucky singer Cliff Carlisle, who later recorded with him, taped this recollection in an interview with Eugene Earle.

> He crossed that leg — well, his leg didn't do like mine does; my leg won't hang down... he put one leg over the other, and it was hanging right down... and he opened that mouth — and he had a long face, you know, long jaw, like; anyhow, it just flopped! Jimmie reminded me more of a coloured person, or a negro, or whatever you want to call them... than anybody I ever saw.[10]

Left, *Jimmie in blackface.* Above, *on tour with a Hawaiian outfit.*

Carrie was not overjoyed at Jimmie travelling with what she called a 'shabby little medicine show', but he was able to support himself and send a little money home. And, more importantly, the fresh, dry mountain air was helping his damaged lungs. Jimmie was also gaining experience in dealing with audiences, mixing with other musicians, and absorbing new musical experiences and influences which would widen his style and repertoire. The money he sent home was saved by Carrie, for despite his wishes she was working herself, at the newsstand at the Union Station on the nightshift. In late summer, Jimmie left the medicine circuit and joined a tent show playing at the larger towns. He even bought a share in the show; and then, realising that a good profit could be made, he bought out the owners completely. In the early autumn, he sold the show and bought a travelling Hawaiian show and carnival, sinking all his profits in the venture. Touring through Indiana, freak winds completely wrecked the carnival. Flat broke, he was forced to return to Meridian. His venture into the tent show business had proved a disaster; but at least his health was temporarily repaired and he was now able to contemplate a return to his 'real job' — railroading.

According to Carrie Rodgers, it was after this that Jimmie found work on the Florida and East Coast Railroad: which she would seem to place in early 1926. However, the New Orleans and North Eastern letter of recommendation has stated that it was in January 1925 that he headed west 'seaking employment'. Thus, although we can be certain of the date that he left the NO&NE and Meridian, there is considerable uncertainty as to exactly where he went. Porterfield is of the opinion that he did, in fact, go west and found work on the Southern Pacific Railroad. In the course of this job, he worked in Utah and Colorado — which Mrs Rodgers claims happened in 1924. Porterfield has suggested that the Florida experience followed on from the destruction of his carnival in that state, for the freak winds could well have been a Florida tornado.[11] The affair is further complicated by the recollections of Albert Fullam, who worked with Jimmie in his railroad days. Fullam recorded the following reminiscences:

> When I first met Jimmie Rodgers, it was at Meridian, Mississippi, in the spring of 1927 ... I got to know him pretty well ... I said 'I think I'm going to the Florida East Coast, they're hiring men down there right now.' And he said, 'Well, I'll mark off and go with you.'[12]

Fullam is obviously mistaken about the date of his first meeting with Rodgers; but if it were 1925, it would certainly fit both the letter and Carrie's account. Because of the lack of conclusive evidence, this must remain highly speculative, and the actual sequence of events may never be known. However, it is our opinion that Carrie's recollections, with the exception of her dates, are, in this instance, correct. There is a certain ring of authenticity about the personal details of her account. But it should be remembered that this is only conjectural, and furthermore that, owing to the many serious errors in Fullam's story, little reliance can be placed upon it. However, let us then assume that Jimmie left the New Orleans and North Eastern in January 1925, intending to head west. Then he heard that the Florida and East Coast were hiring men and travelled there instead.

The new job meant living in Miami, where the Rodgerses set up home in a shabby apartment. For most of the year Jimmie was once again a brakeman; but the soft, damp Florida air and the hard, gruelling work again undermined his health. Jimmie had a friend in Tucson, Arizona, who had offered to get him a job on the Southern Pacific Line, and both Jimmie and Carrie thought that the dry desert climate would be good for his lungs. While in Miami, they had managed to save some money and now they used this to buy their first car, an old and well-used Dodge. Packing their possessions, they set out on the long drive to Arizona. Jimmie got the job but unfortunately things did not work out as the couple had planned. Carrie has related what happened:

> The Southern Pacific yards in Tucson are known to all experienced railroad men as being about the toughest spot — for a brakeman — in the United States. Mountainous box-cars plunging down steep hills require strong bodies, arms of steel, powerful chests on the men who must control them. Twisting wheels is not enough; brakemen must use what is called the "Brake stick". This requires more strength, more endurance, than a sick boy with wasting lungs can furnish.[13]

But Jimmie held on to the job, for he was a long way from Meridian and almost penniless. One day's work often meant Jimmie needed two days to recover. Carrie realised that he was rapidly killing himself and tried to persuade him to leave the Southern. Jimmie, however, fought against the idea, believing that he would be unable to find another job. But by the end of 1925, he finally had to face the truth — railroad work was too exhausting for a man in his condition. On free railroad passes, they travelled to San Antonio, Texas, where he thought he might find less strenuous work. They spent their last few dollars on a sleeping berth and, arriving in San Antonio, checked into a cheap hotel opposite Sunset Station.

Carrie intended to sell some of her clothes to raise a little cash, but their trunk had gone astray on the journey. Things were now looking quite serious for them. Early next morning, Jimmie went out 'to make the rounds', as he told Carrie. He later returned with two dollars, supposedly from an old friend, but Carrie suspected that he had been busking in the bars and poolrooms of downtown San Antonio. Actually, Jimmie had other ways of raising a dollar when the need arose. One method was related to Jim Evans, president of the Rodgers fan club, by Carrie herself. Jimmie, when really desperate, would buy an expensive guitar or other stringed instrument on credit, and then immediately pawn it and leave the area. However, it is to his credit that he kept a list of all the shops that he had defrauded and eventually repaid them — that is, all except one, whose address he had mislaid.[14]

On another free pass they travelled to Galveston where they claimed the insurance money on Carrie's lost trunk. Jimmie, afraid that they might be stranded in Texas, decided to send Carrie and Anita home to Mississippi while he made one last attempt to find work. Carrie was understandably reluctant to leave her husband alone and ill in Texas, but for the sake of Anita she returned to her parents' home. Jimmie followed her just after Christmas after a fruitless search. He was tired and ill but pleased to be at home with his family. Rest and good food improved his health and for several weeks he took things easy — visiting his brothers and friends and playing music. Probably, by now, Jimmie realised that his railroad days were over, for he apparently never again tried to find a railroad job. After 14 years' service on the rails, that part of his life was over.

By the end of January 1926 Jimmie was growing restless. Carrie suggested that he wait until the weather grew warmer and then join another medicine show. But Jimmie had been in touch with another old friend, Fred Jones, who was now a chief detective in Asheville, North Carolina. Jones had offered Jimmie a job as special agent on the city's payroll. About the end of January or early February, Jimmie set out for the Carolinas. After several weeks he sent for Carrie and Anita to join him.

In the past, it has always been accepted that Jimmie left for Asheville in 1927. However, when one considers that he could not have left Mississippi until February at the earliest, then worked as a 'special agent', then a caretaker, and still formed his band in March, it becomes obvious that he could not possibly have had time for all this activity. It seems more likely, then, that he worked for the police office for a short time, then as a caretaker for the remainder of the year and for part of 1927. We would further suggest that the caretaking work was on a part-time basis and that he was already considering a full-time career in music as early as spring 1926. But at the time of the move to the Carolinas, this was not in his mind.

Carrie, during Jimmie's absences, had begun to take a course in stenography. Nate, her brother, had arranged for her to gain experience in his office. This was unknown to Jimmie for he strongly disapproved of his wife working. But Carrie felt it likely that it would be she who would be the breadwinner of the family. In Asheville, Jimmie was beginning to realise that the job was nothing more than charity on the part of Fred Jones, and that whatever Asheville needed it wasn't a special agent. Even when he was right down on his luck, Jimmie appears to have had a horror of charity. Consequently, he gave up the job. Carrie has also noted that police work was completely alien to Jimmie's nature anyway.

Jimmie found another job almost straight away, as the caretaker for an apartment house. With the job came a rent-free cottage. Apparently it was about this time that he realised he would never work the railroads again, for even his caretaking duties were a severe strain on his health. Despite his wife's attempts to get him to visit a hospital, or even rest for a while, he refused. He grew thinner and began to worry about the future, something he had apparently never done before. As the weather grew milder, and his duties became less arduous, he was able to visit old friends and started to hang around the music shops. One day, Anita let out that her mother was taking the stenographer's course. Jimmie was furious and had no intention of letting his wife work. But he had been making his own plans for the future and now confided to Carrie that he had decided to become a full-time musician, playing wherever people would listen — schoolhouses, picnics, fairs, dances, anywhere. The exact date of this decision is unknown, but we assume it was around April/May 1926, and it seems likely that Jimmie retained the caretaking post until the early spring of the following year. Throughout the summer of '26 the engagements that he played were probably on a semi-professional basis, as and when he could take time off from the apartment house. One engagement we do know about was at Johnson City in the summer of that year, where he met the Tennessee Ramblers (not to be confused with the Tenneva Ramblers who were to become the Jimmie Rodgers Entertainers).

The Tennessee Ramblers were a family group comprising William Sievers (fiddle), his son James (banjo) and daughter Willie (guitar). The line-up was usually augmented by Walter McKinney on steel guitar. The band were from the Oak Ridge area and began their career in 1922. James (Mack) Sievers, interviewed by Charles K. Wolfe in 1973, had this to say about their meeting with Rodgers:

In 1926 Dad got us booked in Johnson City at what they called the Trade Week Program, put on by merchants, run for two weeks. The head man was a fellow named A. D. Ritchey ... He had several entertainers from everywhere and we, as the Tennessee Ramblers, were working each night in a spot on the program. A boy came in there by the name of Jimmie Rodgers, a yodeller. The boy that played with him looked like he was a Cherokee Indian — his name was Ernest Helton — I believe from Glen Rock Station, North Carolina. They'd sit around and practice, this boy played guitar for Jimmie, things like 'Right on down through Birmingham', those nice runs. They went over good, and everybody commented on the easy way Jimmie could yodel ... They were both extremely friendly fellows, and they'd come by where we were practicing and sit in and maybe play one with us ... We never seen Jimmie anymore but some of our friends seen him in Chatanooga shortly after that and said Jimmie asked about us ... That was at Keystone Park in Johnson City ... I remember that a storm blew down part of the grandstand, and I recall, it seems like, that some of the entertainers hardly realised expenses out of the deal.[15]

These fascinating reminiscences raise several interesting points. First, that Jimmie was using a guitarist to accompany him. This would fit in with our assumption that Rodgers was mainly a banjoist until around the time of his first recordings. Whether or not Jimmie was playing banjo with Helton is not known; but it may be that he was only vocalising and used the other man as his sole accompaniment. Little is known about Ernest Helton, but he was involved with other Asheville musicians and that was no doubt where Jimmie first made his acquaintance. The phrase 'those nice runs' would seem to suggest that he was playing the same runs that Jimmie later made so much a part of his own guitar style. Yet this in itself is curious, for Helton recorded for Okeh in 1925, and for Paramount the year before, as a banjo player. The second point is the storm which wrecked the grandstand. Could this possibly have any connection with the story about the storm (hurricane?) which supposedly wrecked Jimmie's own tent show some time earlier?

Because of the lack of evidence to the contrary, we can only assume that Jimmie went back to his caretaking work for the winter of '26/27, but was now set on a career in music. He told Carrie that he wanted to pick up some musicians as a backing group, men who could play 'his sort of music'. Presumably he felt that a band sound would be more successful for the type of engagement he had been playing. However, with regard to the formation of the band there are many discrepancies between the account of Carrie Rodgers and the more recent research of Dave Samuelson.

According to Carrie, Jimmie formed his band before he commenced his full-time career. When Carrie asked him why he didn't want to try it on his own he replied,

> I might get scared — or run out of breath. Anyway my long suit right now is the banjo; and that isn't so hot solo . . . but I'm gonna make that old guitar of mine obey me yet.[16]

Jimmie soon met three young musicians, Jack and Claude Grant and Jack Pierce, formed a band called the Jimmie Rodgers Entertainers, and began his career.

However, according to the research of Dave Samuelson (who has interviewed the only surviving member of the band, Claude Grant), Jimmie Rodgers had already been performing for some time before he met the Grants. Jimmie had certainly played solo over WWNC, and was appearing at a fair in Johnson City, Tennessee, as a popular vocalist and novelty yodeller when he met the band, who were already well known in their home area.[17]

The men with whom Jimmie was to be so briefly associated were all from the city of Bristol on the Tennessee/Virginia border. They had formed a band in the early '20s, and by 1923 they were playing semi-professional engagements in the Bristol area. Claude Grant played guitar and took the lead vocals; his brother played mandolin, and Jack Pierce played fiddle. In 1925 they coined the name Tenneva Ramblers from Bristol's location. Often they were joined by Smokey Davis, a blackface comedian who added comedy sketches to the band's music. The band were based at Pierce's mother's boarding house (a rendezvous for local musicians) and played many engagements in the area. In March 1927 they were booked for the Johnson City fair. Jimmie Rodgers was impressed by the band's music and asked if they would join him as his backing group. They, in turn, were impressed by his boasts of radio success, but nevertheless declined to join him. However, several weeks later they called him from Bristol and accepted. They renamed themselves the Jimmie Rodgers Entertainers and spent some time rehearsing at Rodgers' home in Asheville.

Even before Christmas 1926, Carrie had realised that it would be best for Jimmie if he could find work as a professional musician. Carrie was thinking of a dance orchestra where Jimmie might earn as much as $30 a week without exhausting himself. After seven years of moving around the country, she was feeling the need to settle down somewhere — especially now, as Anita was about to start school. But the main drawback to Jimmie becoming a musician was, as she saw, his inability to read music. Thus she believed there was little hope.

In fact, it seems strange that Jimmie had never considered trying to make a career in music before: especially when one considers his success with Terrell's Comedians, and his later experiences with medicine shows. Perhaps he felt that he lacked the necessary talent, or that his music would not be popular. One assumes, however, that the early records of the Virginia singer Henry Whitter, which acted as a spur to so many other artists, would have had the same effect on Rodgers — and if he was the inveterate record buyer his wife claims he was, he would almost certainly have heard them. Reading between the lines of Carrie's book, one gets the impression that Jimmie was never very happy with his instrumental ability, especially his guitar-playing. So probably, until his ill-health forced him to change his occupation, Jimmie always considered himself a railroader first and foremost, with his music as only a pleasurable hobby.

According to Carrie Rodgers, it was about this time that Jimmie started 'tacking yodels onto everything'.[18] But Jimmie had developed his yodel long before this and one assumes that she means he started adding yodels to many different kinds of songs. Interestingly, Goebel Reeves, whom Jimmie had met in 1923, claimed that he had taught Jimmie to yodel while another mutual friend had taught him to play guitar.[19] However, other musicians who had known Rodgers before this have testified that he was yodelling as early as 1920. Thanks to the research of blues authority David Evans, we have the recollections of black musicians who knew Rodgers at this time.

While Rodgers was farming in Purvis, Mississippi in 1921, he met Herb Quinn, a black farmer and string band musician. When interviewed by Evans, Quinn recalled —

> He [Rodgers] had just started out then . . . he was married and his wife was named Lady. You know he had a song of that. See, he hollered 'Oh, My Lady'. That was his wife's name.[20]

As Evans points out, Quinn is confused, and obviously trying to make sense of Rodgers' yodelling refrain. The Rev. Rubin Lacy is another who remembered Rodgers yodelling in the 1920s. Lacy thought that Rodgers just invented his yodel; he reckoned it to be a gimmick which just came to him. These reminiscences, with Billy Terrell's recollections, make nonsense of Reeves' claims. But Reeves was well-known for his dramatic flair, and for distorting the truth about himself. Thus, although the two men did almost certainly meet, it is doubtful if Reeves actually taught Jimmie anything.

Another point which merits attention here is the origin of the term 'Blue Yodeler'. Carrie Rodgers claims that this was first used in 1927 after the formation of the Entertainers. At one small engagement, she overheard a young girl say to her companion 'That blue yodeler's here', meaning Jimmie. Carrie, not having heard the expression before, felt it to be a perfect billing — ' "Jimmie Rodgers, Blue Yodeler", a fine way to book himself.'[21] But according to Terrell, Jimmie had called himself a blue yodeller in 1923. Perhaps Terrell is mistaken, but his story has innumerable details which have the ring of truth about them; and it seems as if Carrie is mistaken here. But certainly her story has a pleasant folksy ring about it.

It is also interesting to consider how Jimmie Rodgers developed his particular style of yodelling. He was not the first country musician to

Roosevelt Holts and Herb Quinn, Mississippians who remember Rodgers.

record a yodel, for Riley Puckett had done this three years before (*Rock All Our Babies To Sleep* [Columbia 107-D]). But what Rodgers developed was, apparently, a unique yodelling refrain, owing some debt to two sources: the Afro-American falsetto 'blue note' and Swiss-style yodelling. How far it is possible to label Rodgers a 'blues singer' and exactly how much his music owes to black blues are points which we will discuss in Chapter 7; but certainly the origins of his highly original blue yodel are, we believe, deep in the Afro-American tradition.

Traditional black music had long employed falsetto singing, developed no doubt from the field-holler of ante-bellum days. This falsetto was incorporated into blues music and many recorded examples could be cited. One interesting example which demonstrates a tangled web of relationships with Jimmie Rodgers is by the influential Mississippi blues singer Tommy Johnson. Johnson recorded several pieces which featured his curious and distinctive falsetto. One title, *Cool Drink of Water Blues* (Victor 21279), has him singing a falsetto refrain of 'Lord, Lord, Lord' in a style very reminiscent of Jimmie's yodel. Ishman Bracey, an associate of Johnson who recorded at the same sessions, and also employed falsetto, worked as a water boy on the Illinois Central Line in his youth and knew Rodgers well in the early '20s. When interviewed by Evans he was careful to point out that the yodel he had learned as a boy was very different

Tommy Johnson (left) *and Ishman Bracey.*

from the one later recorded by Rodgers.[22] Evans thinks it likely that Rodgers and Tommy Johnson met at some time. However, it would be foolish to assume that the two men were influenced by each other on the basis of only one recorded example. Far more likely that both Rodgers and Johnson were influenced by common sources. It seems probable to us that Rodgers, through his contacts with black musicians, was influenced by their falsetto notes and somehow combined this with certain elements of the Swiss style. Thus was his famous 'blue yodel' born.

Meanwhile, in the spring of 1927, Rodgers was organising his band. Details of their style and repertoire are tantalisingly absent. The later recordings of the band, without Rodgers, show a repertoire of the usual mixture of traditional ballads, popular items and some original or rearranged material, usually by Claude Grant, performed within the standard string band style. However, the blending of mandolin and fiddle produces a curious, distinctive harmony which gives the band a unique sound. The best-known photograph of the band with Rodgers, dated May 1927, was taken in Asheville. It shows the members playing instruments with which they were not usually associated — except Rodgers, who holds a tenor banjo. It seems likely that Jimmie did use banjo more than guitar with the Entertainers. We can assume, however, that he used guitar for his solo spots, as two songs that he was featuring at this time were *T for Texas* and *Sleep, Baby, Sleep,* neither of which lends itself to solo banjo accompaniment.

In May the band made their first radio broadcast. The Asheville Chamber of Commerce sponsored its own show over WWNC — Wonderful Western North Carolina — which advertised local beauty spots. Through the efforts of Fred Jones, the Entertainers were given a spot on the show. Carrie was surprised when she discovered they were not being paid for their services, and Jimmie explained that they needed the publicity, and radio meant they would reach the widest possible audience. The programme ran twice weekly, but the Entertainers received little attention. They did receive some fan mail, but even so were dropped after only one

Left, *Rodgers and Claude Grant*. Above, *the Jimmie Rodgers Entertainers:* (standing) *Rodgers, Jack Pierce*, (seated) *Jack and Claude Grant. Both photographs were taken in Asheville about May 1927.*

month. The Asheville papers carried advertisements for the show and despite the fact that Jimmie's name appeared as 'Rogers', both he and Carrie got quite a kick from seeing his name in print. But all were disappointed that the band had received so little attention. Carrie later found out that the noted North Carolina journalist Walter Wamboldt had rung the station to find out more about Jimmie, only to be told, 'He isn't anybody; just a bum'.[23] But after the WWNC interlude, Jimmie could at least book the Entertainers as 'Popular Radio Artists'.

On the whole, the band were a failure in Asheville. They played only one engagement in the city and drew only small crowds in the surrounding villages. Rodgers and Claude Grant went on alone to Marion, North Carolina, to try to find some more bookings. They were unlucky there, but were able to persuade the owner of the luxurious North Fork Mountain Resort to hire them. The band were booked to appear during dinner and at weekend dances for $180.00 a week plus room and board. The engagement lasted six weeks. It was also at this time that Jimmie received replies from the Victor and Brunswick record companies. He had written earlier in the year seeking a recording audition. Both companies thanked him for his offer but pointed out they had all the rural talent they needed.

From the time the band left Asheville until they recorded for Victor in early August, the two main sources give conflicting accounts of the events. According to Carrie, she accompanied Jimmie to North Fork leaving Anita in Asheville with friends. She has said that she regretted leaving there for they had made many acquaintances. After the booking ended, the Entertainers took to the road in the Grants' battered old sedan. Throughout July, the band played whenever and wherever people would listen. According to Carrie, Jimmie's solos 'stopped the show', and probably in view of later events she is right. But on the whole they found little work, and one is tempted to speculate why. After all, the band were popular before Rodgers joined them, and after the split they remained popular and were still active in the music field until World War II. Was it that the band and Rodgers were so ill-matched? One would scarcely believe it: the band was certainly talented, and Jimmie, as some of his later records demonstrated, could make a good sound with even the most inappropriate accompaniment. Perhaps the answer is that in the Carolinas there were so many fine string bands that the Entertainers couldn't get in. It is likely that a local outfit like Charlie Poole's or Clay Everhard's would draw the support of Carolina audiences. But whatever the explanation, the July of 1927 was tough going for the band. At the end of the month, Carrie had to remain behind at a small hotel as security for the unpaid bill while the band went off in search of more bookings. While they were gone, Carrie heard from a local storekeeper that the Victor company was holding auditions in Bristol, Tennessee. Frantically she tried to contact her husband. Finally, in the early hours of the morning, Jimmie arrived having heard of the auditions elsewhere.

However, according to Samuelson's research, the Entertainers were still at North Fork when Jimmie and Jack Pierce went to Bristol to persuade Pierce's father to put up the money for another second-hand car for use as band transport. When they arrived they found far more musicians than

A rare photograph of the Jimmie Rodgers Entertainers at the North Fork Mountain Resort, about July 1927. Left to right, *Pierce, Claude Grant, Rodgers, Jack Grant.*

usual at the boarding house and it was from them that Rodgers and Pierce learned about the Victor auditions. Rodgers saw Ralph Peer, who was in charge of the session, and told him about the band. Peer advised him to bring them to Bristol for a try-out. They picked up the Grants from North Fork and collected Carrie and Anita from Asheville (where they had remained since the Entertainers began the North Fork booking, according to this source), and arrived back in Bristol on 2 August.

It seems strange that the two accounts of these events are so different. From the second source, Carrie's recollections of busking through the Carolinas in July is missing. But then the whole episode of Rodgers' relationship with the Entertainers has been frequently distorted, and after so many years it is doubtful if the real facts will ever be known. But whatever the truth, one thing is certain: the Bristol auditions were to change Jimmie's life completely. After seven years of bad luck and hard times, he was finally about to lose those brakeman's blues.

3 / No Hard Times

Gonna buy all my children a brand new pair of shoes
I'm gonna quit singing these doggone hard time blues.

(No Hard Times)

Bristol occupies a unique location for it straddles the border of two states, Virginia and Tennessee; the main street (appropriately named State Street) is the state line. Bristol, in its country music context, has often been romanticised as a rural village, but even in the mid-'20s it was a sophisticated provincial city with up-to-date amenities and boasting two daily newspapers. Nevertheless, for all its modern developments, the city and its surrounding area was a fertile one for country music performers, and it was to Bristol that Ralph Peer brought Victor's portable recording machines in the summer of 1927. It was to be one of the most significant field recording sessions in the history of hillbilly music, and the watershed in the life of the tubercular ex-railroader Jimmie Rodgers.

Ralph Peer, together with other early pioneers of the industry such as Frank Walker, Art Satherley and Polk Brockman, occupies an important place in the development of recorded country music, for without the foresight and faith of such men the popularisation and the subsequent wide commercial recording of the music would never have occurred. Although, as later events have demonstrated, there was a considerable market for hillbilly records (not confined to the rural South), the recording companies were unaware of it, or perhaps chose to ignore it, until it was forcibly brought to their attention. These companies were based in the North — Chicago or New York — and were far from the scene of the action; and they might never have entered the field to the extent that they did, had it not been for their perspicacious talent scouts, who gambled on the commercial potential of this as yet unknown quantity, country music. Of all these pioneers, perhaps Ralph Peer is the most important, the prime mover in making 'country' a recognised branch of the music industry.

Peer came from Independence, Missouri, the son of a storekeeper. While still in his teens, he worked in his father's store selling records. At the end of World War I, he moved to New York and began to work for the Okeh Record Company. It was here, on 14 February 1920, that he assisted in the recording of *That Thing Called Love* (Okeh 4113) by Mamie Smith. The record, generally accepted as the first of the so-called race records, set off the whole business of ethnic recordings by commercial concerns. Then, in June 1923, Peer's recording of Fiddlin' John Carson sparked off the white equivalent of race recordings — hillbilly music. As Peer has described the events:

> In 1921 [*sic*] quite by accident, I unearthed and developed the business of recording negro artists to make records for sale to the colored population. Two years later I had the good fortune to stumble across the fact that throughout the Southern States there existed a separate and distinct repertoire of popular music, not connected in any way with the productions of New York and Chicago songwriters.[1]

In his 'good fortune', Peer was helped in no small measure by Polk Brockman, an Atlanta, Georgia, businessman and record dealer. It was probably Brockman who first realised that there was a potential market for rural music in general, and for a recording by an obscure jockey-turned-fiddler in particular. It was this realisation that led Brockman to contact Okeh Records, and brought about Peer's field-recording of two fiddle tunes by John Carson.

It was almost certainly Peer who coined the name 'hillbilly' as a description of the music. Archie Green's work on this aspect is invaluable and the enquiring reader is strongly recommended it.[2] Here it is sufficient to say that the term 'hillbilly' had been a fairly common expression from about 1900 onwards, as a description for a native of the Ozark mountains. The term has abusive connotations, similar to 'hick' or 'clodhopper'. However, in January 1925, Ralph Peer had recorded a group of musicians from Wautauga County, North Carolina. At the end of the session Peer asked for the group's name. Al Hopkins, the leader, told him they had no official name and were just a bunch of hillbillies from Carolina. He suggested Peer think up a name and the latter listed them as The Hill Billies. Thus was the term born, and within a year or so it had come to describe the music itself.

In 1927 Ralph Peer left Okeh and started in business for himself as a song publisher. He arranged a partnership with the giant Victor record company. As Peer has put it,

> In 1927 I decided to go into business for myself, and thus I became a music publisher. At that time, the world's largest manufacturer of phonograph records — the Victor Talking Machine Company — had not been successful in its efforts to enter the hillbilly field. When I offered to bring them the necessary artists and repertoire so that they might try out the possibilities, they quickly accepted my offer and a business alliance was started which continued for many years.[3]

It is worth mentioning here that even though Victor may have been hesitant to enter the hillbilly field, they were not, as Peer has suggested, unsuccessful. They recorded probably the first hillbilly record in 1922 (Eck Robertson and Henry Gilliland) and numbered Vernon Dalhart, Kelly Harrell, Carson Robison, Jules Allen and Carl Sprague amongst their country performers. Dalhart's 1924 record of *The Prisoner's Song/Wreck of the Old 97* was a terrific seller by any standard. However, their ventures into the field were certainly more widespread once Peer had joined them. In return for locating the talent and supervising the recordings for Victor, he was to have the copyrights to the material published through his own company, Southern Music. Peer then began a series of historic recording sessions throughout the rural South, where hasty and temporary field recording studios were set up to audition and record local performers. In this manner, many of the most important and influential country music performers were discovered. In the summer of 1927, Ralph Peer came to Bristol.

> During the spring of 1928 [*sic*] I made a survey of various Southern cities and determined to make initial recordings for Victor in Atlanta, Savannah, Bristol, Tenn., and Memphis. A recording crew of two men was assigned to me and I set about the business of finding talent and repertoire.[4]

Peer is obviously mistaken about the date, for it was 1927, and even so, must have been the very early part of that year, for in February he was actually recording in Memphis where he had discovered and named the Carolina Tar Heels: Dock Walsh and Gwen Foster.

Although Peer has stated that the object of this trip was to find talent, he had already ensured that the sessions would not be a complete waste if local performers failed to audition, or if they were not of suitable ability. At each location Peer had arranged recording dates for established Victor performers. In Bristol, for example, he had organised a date for the Virginian singer Ernest V. Stoneman, an already well-known and successful performer.

The whole subject of the Bristol sessions and Jimmie Rodgers has long been a matter for speculation, and the events are open to a wide variety of interpretations. The sources for these events are often conflicting, and

Ralph Peer.

many problems need to be re-examined. One such problem – whether or not Ralph Peer actually advertised these auditions – can now be solved, thanks to the recent research of Charles K. Wolfe.

For some considerable time it had been accepted that Peer had advertised in local papers for talent for these field auditions. But when country music grew into a legitimate branch of academic study, these advertisements were not to be found by scholarly investigation. This led Ed Kahn to claim that in his extensive research on Peer and the Carter Family (another Bristol discovery) he had been unable to find any corroboration for Peer's claim of advertising.[5] However, Wolfe's more recent research has now seemingly solved this problem; for Peer used a subtle and inexpensive form of advertising, making sure that local performers were aware that he was looking for talent. We suggest that the sequence of events, from his arrival in Bristol, was as follows.

Peer, his wife and the two engineers arrived in Bristol on 21 or 22 July, and set up a temporary studio in the Taylor-Christian Building on the Tennessee side of State Street. The building had been used for many purposes, but at that time was standing empty. Peer was interviewed by a reporter from the Bristol *Herald-Courier* and a brief article appeared in the edition for 24 July (Sunday) under the headline 'Record Engineers Locate In Bristol'. The story continued that Peer would record 'well-known native talent'[6] – obviously a reference to the forthcoming Stoneman session. In the same edition of the paper appeared what at first glance seems to be the famous advertisement. However, inspection reveals that this was put out by a local store, Clark-Jones-Sheeley, a furniture shop and Victor agent. It might or might not be construed as an appeal for local talent, but seems more like an invitation to watch a technical demonstration of the recording session. But regardless of its original intent, it did not attract performers and Peer cast around for more direct publicity.

> In Bristol, the problem [of finding talent and repertoire] was not easy because of the relatively small population in that area. The local broadcasting stations, music stores, record dealers, etc. helped me as much as possible, but few candidates appeared.[7]

Peer had recorded Stoneman on Monday and Ernest Phipps on Tuesday. On Wednesday, 27 July, he thought of the solution to his problem of finding talent.

> I then appealed to the editor of a local paper, explaining to him the great advantages to the community of my enterprise. He thought that I had a good idea and ran half a column on his front page.[8]

The column mentioned by Peer appeared in the *News Bulletin* (afternoon edition) for that day, under the heading: 'Mountain Songs Recorded Here By Victor Co.'[9]

The article goes on to describe those whom Peer had already recorded. As Charles Wolfe has summarised:

Don't deny yourself the sheer joy of Orthophonic music

A SMALL down-payment puts this great musical instrument in your home. Here is a source of entertainment for yourself and friends without end. You may have it now for a little cash and nominal monthly payments.

The Victor Co. will have a recording machine in Bristol for 10 days beginning Monday to record records—Inquire at our Store.

Clark-Jones-Sheeley Co.

Victrolas — Records — Sheet Music
621 State St. Bristol, Va.

The New Orthophonic **Victrola**

The building used by Victor for the Bristol sessions. Their studio was on the top floor.

This, then, is the famous 'ad' that Peer ran whose existence has been questioned by scholars. It was not a formal ad, but rather a news story which acted as an advertisement.[10]

The following day, Thursday, the local talent began to arrive: the Johnson Brothers, Blind Alfred Reed, the Carter Family, El Watson and Jimmie

Rodgers. According to Peer he was 'deluged with groups of singers who had not visited Bristol in their entire lifetime arriving by bus, horse and buggy, trains, or on foot'.[11] A picturesque and folksy record of the arrival of the Carter Family has been left by Gladys Millard:

> On July 31st, 1927 Daddy loaded up the old A model with the harp, guitar, Mother, Maebelle, Joe, my 7-month-old brother . . . and me, a little eight-year-old girl . . . We all took off for Bristol . . . It took us almost the whole day to get the 25 miles from our house to Bristol. Dirt roads all the way, creeks to cross and poor Daddy had three flat tyres . . . . We got to Aunt Vergie's house about dark. She lived in Bristol. That would give us the night to rest, tune the instruments, rehearse the songs.[12]

How Jimmie Rodgers came to the session is another matter of argument. Peer has stated that Rodgers phoned him from Asheville on Thursday, 27 July. Rodgers had told Peer about his band and Peer had told him to come in for an audition in a week's time. However, as we mentioned in the previous chapter, Samuelson has suggested that Rodgers and Jack Pierce had heard about the auditions while visiting Bristol itself. Mrs Rodgers' account confirms that Jimmie was not in Asheville at this time. Thus it is our guess that Rodgers was in Bristol when he heard about the auditions, and phoned Peer on a local call. Peer, throughout his 1953 article, frequently makes quite serious errors and it would have been easy for him to confuse a long-distance with a local call. There is another interesting point regarding this: Clayton McMichen, the Georgia fiddler with whom Rodgers later recorded, claimed that he introduced Rodgers to Ralph Peer in Atlanta in 1926 or 1927. The story has little to commend it and is not reported in any other source, though it is possible that Jimmie visited Atlanta at this time and may have known McMichen. Anyway, early in August Jimmie Rodgers and the Entertainers arrived in Bristol.

The Rodgerses found accommodation over a baker's shop on State Street. From the window they could see the Taylor-Christian building where Ralph Peer was holding those all-important auditions. According to Carrie Rodgers, the party arrived early in the morning and auditioned the same day; most other sources put their audition on the day following their arrival. She relates that after Jimmie and the band had arranged the audition, her husband returned to their rooms highly elated. He saw some significance in the names Victor and Peer. As he said to Carrie,

> Victor — Peer. Sort of looks to me like those two names would be pretty nice for me to be connected with. A victor is a winner isn't he? And a peer is top of the heap.[13]

Carrie teased him over this and suggested that he should change his name to something like Jimmie Starr. More seriously, they then discussed which numbers they should perform. Carrie was hoping that he might be able to do his solo numbers like *T for Texas* or *The Soldier's Sweetheart,* but she realised that the audition material would have to be band numbers. After an hour or so, Jimmie returned to the Taylor-Christian building for the audition. The band, he told Carrie, were to meet him there.

Shortly afterwards, he returned. Alone and upset he told Carrie:

> The boys have made arrangements with Mr Peer to make a test record without me. I guess I don't blame them. If they go over — if they click — they'll get more. Dividing by three is more per each than dividing by four. And it's like they told me: they worked as a trio before they met me, so they're used to it . . . They've already had an audition, so it's all set for them. They're to record in the morning.[14]

Having delivered this bad news, Jimmie then seemed to have made up his mind to go it alone: to pressure Peer into giving him a solo audition. Carrie agreed that this was the only thing left to do and forced Jimmie to take a pocketful of his fan letters with him to show Peer: presumably, to demonstrate that he already had some following. She was also hoping that he would give Peer *T for Texas,* which she considered his best song.

When he had gone, she watched from the window. After a while she noticed Jimmie signalling from a window on the other side of the street. He seemed to be asking her for matches to light his cigarette. She grabbed a box and dashed into the corridor where she met Anita and Lottie Mae Mixon, Jimmie's half sister. Lottie Mae had been on her way to visit them in Asheville, but a wire from Carrie had brought her on to Bristol. Together, they all went over to the temporary studio. Here they found a pleased Jimmie just about to listen to the replay of his first recording, *Sleep, Baby, Sleep.* Jimmie explained to them that he hadn't needed a light but just wanted his wife and daughter with him at that proud moment of his life. Carrie was of course pleased about the recordings, but felt that Jimmie had made a mistake in his selection of numbers. Even when Peer asked Jimmie for an original composition Jimmie sang *The Soldier's Sweetheart* instead of *T for Texas.* When Jimmie finished, Carrie asked Peer if Jimmie could do one more song.

> Oh please — let him make another record. He didn't give you 'T for Texas' — and that's the one everybody's crazy about. It shows what he can really do.[15]

Peer, according to this account, replied that it was his ironclad rule never to record more than two tests for any artist. However, he did give Jimmie $20 and had him sign a short-term contract: an option on Jimmie's services for another recording session if the first record should prove successful. The Rodgerses returned to the barber's shop. The long wait to see if Jimmie would make it as a recording artist now began.

Thus Carrie Rodgers' account of the events in Bristol in the summer of 1927. Although vivid and with details that smack of authenticity, it does not, unfortunately, match with the other accounts. The main problems are

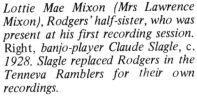

Lottie Mae Mixon (Mrs Lawrence Mixon), Rodgers' half-sister, who was present at his first recording session. Right, *banjo-player Claude Slagle, c. 1928. Slagle replaced Rodgers in the Tenneva Ramblers for their own recordings.*

the split between Rodgers and the Tenneva Ramblers and the exact pattern of the test sessions.

Claude Grant's account, as told to Samuelson, runs as follows. The Tenneva Ramblers and Rodgers auditioned for Peer early on 3 August 1927. They did some duets, Claude Grant sang a solo, and Rodgers sang *T for Texas* with the full band. Peer was impressed, and said he would record the group the next day. They then all went to Mrs Pierce's boarding-house to rehearse and determine the name the group would use on the records. Rodgers wanted 'The Jimmie Rodgers Entertainers', but the rest of the band preferred 'The Tenneva Ramblers' with a subcredit for whoever sang. As a compromise Rodgers came up with 'Jimmie Rodgers and the Grant Brothers', but the trio were unwilling to let anyone get top billing and rejected it. Thus deadlocked, Rodgers and the Ramblers amiably parted company.

Grant believes this argument was only an excuse for Rodgers to break away from the band, noting that Rodgers lost no time in asking Peer if he could record a couple of numbers by himself. He also claims that pressure from Carrie Rodgers was a factor influencing the split.

The Ramblers now called banjoist Claude Slagle at his cab stand and asked if he would record with them on the following day. Slagle had played with the Grants and Pierce many times, and only a few hours' rehearsal were necessary that evening.

On the next day, then — 4 August — Rodgers had his two-song session (at 1.30 pm), and the Ramblers appeared later, at 8.00 pm, to make their three recordings.

Some confirmation of this account may be read into Peer's later statement:

> When I was alone with Jimmie in our recording studio . . . I was elated when I heard him perform without the unsuitable accompaniment . . . sticking to the established facts, I let him record his own song.[16]

This suggests that Peer had definitely heard Jimmie and the Ramblers playing together, despite Carrie's claim to the contrary.

On the reason for the split, Jimmie's assertion (reported by Carrie) that the Ramblers were anxious to secure a three-way rather than four-way division of the recording fee does not stand up to examination; immediately after the breakup, the Ramblers contacted Slagle to make their numbers up to four again. There is more to be said for the theory that Peer advised Jimmie to record solo because the Ramblers were unsuitable accompanists. As well as the statement cited above, Peer's recollections include this passage:

> When Jimmie arrived with his group it was apparent that they were not accustomed to working together. Actually, Jimmie had talked the string band into making the trip from near Asheville to provide himself with transportation, and because he was under the impression that he would need more accompaniment for recording than his own guitar. There was no time for long rehearsals and anyway I had the feeling that a string band accompaniment would be incongruous. Jimmie was quite disappointed when I started to work with the string band, and asked him to come back in the evening for a special session.[17]

However, Jimmie and the Ramblers *had* been playing together for some time. Moreover, as an inveterate record-buyer Jimmie would have known that many singers recorded very successfully with only their own guitar accompaniment. Furthermore, Peer's judgement that 'a string band accompaniment would be incongruous' hardly squares with his later practices at Rodgers' sessions, when he employed accompanying groups including not only string instruments but musical saw and various brass and wind instruments. Finally, this hypothesis asks us to believe that Peer considered Rodgers, from that first hearing, to be a potential top-selling artist; but, as we hope to show, this was not the case. Altogether this theory has too many flaws to be probable, and we are left with the conclusion — which is Claude Grant's claim — that Rodgers and the Ramblers quarrelled the day before they were to record.

In his 1953 article Peer gave the impression that he realised Rodgers had great potential and talent even at his first test recording.

> It seemed to me that he had his own personal and peculiar style, and I thought that his yodel alone might spell success. Very definitely he was worth a trial, and he deserved my close personal attention . . . I considered Rodgers to be one of my best bets.[18]

Yet Peer only recorded two songs by Jimmie; even when Carrie pleaded with him to record just one more, Peer's 'ironclad rule' prevented him. This appears nonsensical when one considers that the Carter Family recorded six titles: four on 1 August and two on the 2nd. Alfred Karnes, a tremendously powerful gospel singer from Corbin, Kentucky, also recorded six titles; and even the Tenneva Ramblers cut three titles — *The Longest Train I Ever Saw, Sweet Heaven When I Die* and *Miss Liza, Poor Gal.* It is possible that Jimmie's repertoire might not have seemed sufficient for more recordings at this time, and Peer does hint at this himself, but Rodgers obviously had *Blue Yodel,* and as he had been a professional musician for some time, it is inconceivable that he should not have had at least half-a-dozen good songs. It seems more likely that Peer considered Rodgers just another singer of average ability, or fitted him in at short notice. The success of his first few records and his later phenomenal rise to fame obviously led to Peer's later claims that he had recognised Jimmie's talent from the start. This would seem to be confirmed by two incidents. First, Peer was apparently in no hurry at all to record Jimmie again. And secondly, Peer later claimed to have rushed Jimmie's first record out, when in fact it was released at the same time as the other Bristol material.

The final problem which needs to be dealt with here is why Carrie's book should disagree with the other sources for these events so drastically. We must keep in mind that her original manuscript was prepared less than two years after the shock of her husband's death. She also had to consider the feelings of those who had put so much faith into the career of the 'Singing Brakeman'. And it should further be remembered that Jimmie Rodgers was, and still is, a very commercial property. Still in mourning then, with Victor Records and Southern Music and a host of loyal and devoted friends to consider, Carrie may well have decided to omit anything from her book which she felt would be harmful to the memory of her husband. And, after all, the petty squabble over label billing is of such a trivial nature that no one emerges with dignity. Carrie certainly did omit other facts about Jimmie's life which might have been considered harmful to his image. Ralph Peer and Jimmie were not only business associates, but close personal friends as well, so it is likely that Peer thought the best solution was to claim that he advised Jimmie to record solo. In fact, he may well have realised that this was a wise move quite soon after the recordings, for he was, after all, getting two good recording acts instead of one.

Of course, there is no reason why Carrie's book should be entirely accurate anyway; it was written purely as a popular account of his life and career to satisfy the constant demands of his many fans for information about his life. No one, not even Carrie herself, could have realised that Jimmie's work would be so enduring and so influential. A popular account was all that was required. It is, of course, possible that Carrie Rodgers did not write the book at all; that it was ghosted by an anonymous author using notes prepared by her. If this was the case, then there is little reason to expect the book to be anything other than a highly romanticised popular account of Jimmie's life. It is unfortunate that the main characters in this story are now dead, and it is likely that many mysteries of Jimmie's life will remain unsolved. The only other possible explanation of the inaccuracies of Carrie's story is that she was herself unaware of the truth of these matters: that Jimmie told her only what he wanted her to know. This, however, seems highly unlikely; Carrie was an intelligent and perceptive woman, highly involved in her husband's career. Even if she had been unaware at the time, she would surely have discovered the truth later.

Before we leave the Bristol sessions, something needs to be said regarding Jimmie's choice of audition material — *The Soldier's Sweetheart* and *Sleep, Baby, Sleep*. Neither song has much to commend it. *Sweetheart* is Jimmie's variation on a traditional theme, pleasant but mediocre:

> Once I had a sweetheart, a sweetheart brave and true,
> His hair was dark and curly, his loving eyes were blue,
> He told me that he loved me, and he often proved it so,
> And he often came to see me when the evening sun was low.
>
> (*The Soldier's Sweetheart,* Victor 20864)

But her sweetheart volunteers for that 'awful German war' and eventually a letter from his captain tells her that her 'darling dear was dead'. *Sleep, Baby, Sleep* is a common lullaby, recorded only two years before by Riley Puckett for Columbia. Rodgers sings both songs in a flat, plaintive style with a guitar backing that is simplicity itself. There is some evidence to suggest that Ralph Peer wanted 'original' compositions,[19] or at least songs which could be claimed as originals, and this would explain *Sweetheart,* but the lullaby remains a strange choice, especially in view of Puckett's earlier recording. Unless, of course, that was the very reason Jimmie chose it: to show that whatever had been recorded he could do as well, or better! Certainly this would fit in with his supremely self-confident approach and his 'I'll show 'em' attitude. In any case, Jimmie's voice proved to be extremely suitable for the limited and relatively unsophisticated recording equipment of the day, and this may well explain the fairly satisfactory sales of his first record — a record by a totally unknown performer.

The Tenneva Ramblers had one more session for Victor, and finally recorded for Columbia in November 1928. The Columbia titles were released under the credit 'The Grant Brothers and their Music'. The band continued playing until the Depression, when they found fulltime jobs outside music. However, the Grant Brothers continued to play at dances and local functions throughout the postwar years. After 1950 they played only for their own amusement. Jack Grant died in 1968 but Claude Grant is still alive, the last surviving member of the ill-fated Entertainers.

* * *

Regardless of the eventual outcome of the recordings, the Rodgers family was better off by $20, and they returned to their rooms well pleased with the day's events. Peer, before Jimmie had left the studio, had advised him that it would be a good idea if they moved nearer to Victor's Camden, New Jersey, headquarters in case the company wanted to record him again. The session appears to have given Jimmie and Carrie a considerable boost but the edge was taken from this by Lottie Mae's suggestion that she should take Anita home with her to Geiger. Lottie Mae realised that they needed to move near to New York, and would need time to organise somewhere to live and work for Jimmie. During this time Anita could only be an additional worry for them. If she returned to Alabama, or went to Carrie's parents in Meridian, she would at least be able to start school in time for the new academic year. Anita's schooling was a problem which was causing Carrie great concern. Although it meant losing Anita for a while, Carrie saw the wisdom of Lottie Mae's suggestion and eventually Jimmie reluctantly agreed. It was finally decided that they would leave for Alabama that night. In the midst of their packing, a messenger arrived with a $50 money order from Carrie's sister Annie Nelson. Carrie had written to her earlier telling her about the Bristol trip and their desperate financial situation. Apart from the money, Annie had helped them, unknowingly, with another problem, for she suggested that Jimmie and Carrie stay with her in Washington, D.C. As Washington was reasonably close to Camden, the Rodgerses decided they would go; in fact, they would leave next day.

Before Anita and Lottie Mae left, Jimmie had a sudden desire to be extravagant. Now that he had $70 he felt they could well afford to celebrate his first recording. The whole family trooped out and Jimmie booked a room and private bath in an expensive hotel. Then Anita had to be taken to the station. After a tearful farewell, Jimmie and Carrie returned to their costly accommodation. Outside, Jimmie ran into an old acquaintance, a salesman. Carrie was somewhat amused to hear her husband bragging about his recent experiences:

'I'm under contract to the Victor Phonograph Company. Just made a recording here today.'[20]

The salesman was suitably impressed and promised to buy a copy. He hoped it was the 'Thelma' one (*T for Texas*). Carrie was now even more convinced that Jimmie had made a mistake in not recording this song for Ralph Peer. Later that night they discussed it, and Jimmie convinced her that the songs he had recorded provided a much better selection to show his talent to the Victor executives and to the world at large.

At the time of these recordings Jimmie was quite ill and no doubt the excitement of the sessions had exacerbated his condition. Even so, he refused to rest and they set out the following day for the Washington home of Carrie's relatives, Annie and Alex Nelson. Carrie immediately had a major battle on her hands to persuade Jimmie that she should take a job, something Jimmie still strongly opposed. However, soon after their arrival,

Jimmie returned home one night soaked through after being caught in a rainstorm. The subsequent chill resulted in a high temperature and a need for complete rest. While he was ill, Carrie took a job in the Happiness Tea Room as a waitress. When Jimmie found out he was furious, but eventually relented, realising that he couldn't support his family until he found work.

Carrie's second problem was to make Jimmie see the necessity of warm clothing for the coming winter. She knew that inadequate protection against the harsh Northern winter could mean his death. But Jimmie was loth to spend money on himself. Eventually, Carrie managed to convince him that as a recording artist he needed to look the part of a successful musician. The only work Jimmie had been able to find was in suburban picture-houses, playing as a 'fill-in' between films. This seemed to lend support to Carrie's argument and so Jimmie invested in some new clothes. But despite warm clothing, the autumn and early winter was almost fatal for Jimmie. He had a serious attack of pleurisy, but even when ill and with a high temperature, he refused to stay at home and insisted upon turning up at his engagements.

Since their arrival in Washington, both Jimmie and Carrie had confidently expected another call from Victor, but despite Jimmie's eagle-eyeing the morning post, the call did not come. Eventually his first record was released, on 7 October 1927.[21] It may have been the celebration party that Jimmie threw to mark the record release which resulted in his meeting with the fine steel guitarist and singer Jimmie Tarlton. Tarlton was very much a roamer and at this time was temporarily resident in Washington. Apart from yodelling it would not appear that the two singers had much in common, and even Tarlton's yodel was more akin to the pure Afro-American falsetto.

Despite his initial excitement, Jimmie was canny enough to hang around the record stores to see how the disc was selling. To his eye it seemed to be going well, but even so, there was still no word from Victor. Ralph Peer, in his 1953 article, did claim that he had tried to get in touch with Rodgers but was unsuccessful. However, as we explain later, we believe that Ralph Peer confused the events of Jimmie's second and third recording sessions, and so his attempt to get in touch with Rodgers could also be misremembered.[22] During November, Jimmie made up his mind that if the Victor people hadn't contacted him by the end of the month, he'd get in touch with them.

It was about this time that he borrowed some money from Carrie, telling her that he had lost heavily in a dice game and owed a friend. In fact he used it to send for Anita, and her arrival came as a pleasant shock for Carrie. Delighted that the whole family was once again together, she immediately set about getting Anita into a Washington school.

Jimmie had made up his mind to go up to New York to find out what was happening about his recordings. The Rodgerses had little spare cash but Carrie scraped together the train-fare and $10 for his living expenses. When Jimmie arrived in New York, with typical recklessness, he booked into the expensive Menger Hotel, even though he hadn't enough money to pay the bill. But, as he later explained to his wife, he knew that Victor would pay his expenses if he recorded for them; and with true self-confidence, he was convinced they would record him. Interestingly, Jimmie himself was now wondering if he hadn't made a mistake by not recording *T for Texas* at his first session. Now, if Victor did record him, he'd made up his mind that the song would be committed to wax — much to Carrie's satisfaction.

Jimmie phoned Ralph Peer from the hotel and told him that if the company were interested in more recordings, he just happened to be in New York for a few days.[23] Peer was interested and arranged for a session on 30 November at the Camden studios. This was almost certainly the day following Jimmie's call. Peer wanted Jimmie to cut four titles at this session. Victor's main studio at Camden was the old Trinity Baptist Church, erected in 1872 but abandoned because of serious structural faults. However, because of its peculiar acoustics, it proved to be ideal for recordings and Victor used it for many years. To the famous old church, then, came Jimmie Rodgers.

The first title of the session, *Ben Dewberry's Final Run,* echoed his railroad background and was the first of his many railroad songs. The song had been written by Rev. Andrew Jenkins, a prolific hillbilly composer. On the recording Jimmie plays one of his best guitar solos, one later to be repeated note-for-note by Hank Snow on his recording of *The Hobo's Last Ride.* The second title was a reworking of an 1893 popular ballad, *Mother Was A Lady.* But it was the final titles which, when released as a coupling, were to establish Rodgers as one of Victor's best selling artists. *T for Texas,* issued as *Blue Yodel,* was the story of 'poor Thelma'. The reverse was *Away Out on the Mountain,* written by Kelly Harrell, a fine singer and textile mill worker from Virginia. Harrell had probably intended to record the song himself with his own Virginia String Band, but Peer suggested that he give it to Rodgers. Unless Harrell was present in the studio at the time of Rodgers' recording, it would seem that Peer had either been in touch with Rodgers before, or had been saving the song against the time when Rodgers did contact him. If the latter, Jimmie learned the song very quickly; he could not read music, so someone must have taught it to him. But it was the first *Blue Yodel* which was to set the scene for Jimmie's best and probably most important group of recordings.

In form, it is a typical blues, a twelve-bar stanza of three lines, with the pattern AAB:

T for Texas, T for Tennessee,
T for Texas, T for Tennessee,
T for Thelma, the girl that made a wreck out of me.

(Blue Yodel, Victor 21142)

The only difference between this and a thousand race records is Jimmie's use of the yodel, for each verse is followed by his blue yodel refrain. In all, Jimmie was to record thirteen Blue Yodels and some twenty-five stylistically related songs.

All the titles from this second session had Jimmie's guitar as their only accompaniment. The *Blue Yodel* coupling (Victor 21142) sold so well that

Kelly Harrell's royalties as composer of *Away Out on the Mountain* earned him $985.00 as his first payment.[24]

Mrs Rodgers remembered that before the session Ralph Peer told Jimmie to give his best during the recordings as 'The professional life of a recording artist was never more than three years'.[25] Jimmie optimistically took this as meaning that Victor would be needing his services for at least the next three years, but Carrie viewed it in another way. She felt that however many records Jimmie made, there would be little profit; after three years he would be back where he started before Bristol. She felt that there would never be a time when they would be financially secure. This view was dramatically reinforced by the arrival of Jimmie's first, and eagerly awaited, royalty cheque, $27 and a few cents for three months' sales. Carrie wondered just how three people could live on $27 every three months. Even Jimmie was depressed at this small amount and for once his usual high spirits were dampened. Carrie did her best to cheer him, and true to form, Jimmie was soon back to his happy-go-lucky, optimistic self. But, as Carrie later found out, Jimmie's cheque represented the largest royalty payment to a 'beginning solo artist on the Victor lists'.[26]

Christmas 1927 was in many ways a far happier occasion for the Rodgerses than any earlier one. True, they still did not have a home of their own, and they were still dependent upon the generosity of relatives. But even so they were together as a family, Jimmie had made three records, and he was working regularly at engagements around Washington and had even managed to broadcast on WTFF. Christmas 1927 was a happy time for Jimmie and Carrie Rodgers, and there was every chance that in 1928 things might get even better.

4 / Jimmie the Kid

> He rode freight trains from east to west
> Now he's fixed himself up nice;
> He's got a beautiful home all of his own,
> It's the yodeler's paradise.
>
> (*Jimmie the Kid*)

1928 was the year that was to see Jimmie Rodgers emerge from the ranks of obscure, struggling hillbilly singers to the pinnacle of fame and popularity; the year in which he was to become a nationally known recording artist, and one of Victor's best-selling performers. Over the next five years Jimmie would set a pattern for young country music singers which few would fail to follow. His influence would endure for many years beyond the remainder of his own brief lifetime, and would contribute significantly towards raising country music from semi-professional to star-orientated status, and place it firmly on the road towards the million-dollar industry with which we are now familiar.

In February 1928 Jimmie was again called to the Camden studios to record. For his previous sessions he had mostly been content to draw upon material with which he was already familiar. His first recordings, with the exception of Kelly Harrell's *Away Out on the Mountain,* were either his own compositions or songs he had been featuring in his act for some time. Now, however, he began a conscious search for material suitable for recording. And it should be remembered that a song which is successful in a stage act does not necessarily make a successful recording. In early February this search for material was becoming urgent, as Victor no longer required just a couple of songs, but planned a session of eight to ten titles. One avenue of help for Jimmie was his sister-in-law Elsie McWilliams. Interviewed some years later, she recalled Jimmie's letter asking for assistance:

> After he made his first records he wrote me that he was in need of some original ballads. Well, I fixed up several that I thought were pretty good, but only one of the lot was accepted.[1]

Ralph Peer phoned Jimmie in early February and was assured that the singer had 'a wealth of new songs'. Recording dates on the 14th and 15th were arranged. When Peer wrote about this session in 1953, he mistakenly referred to it as the second, but from the titles that he claims were recorded, he is obviously referring to this third date.[2] Peer met Rodgers in Philadelphia and together they travelled on to New York, where Jimmie booked into the expensive Walt Whitman Hotel — another indulgence of his liking for 'rich living' and another costly expense sheet for Victor. For the session, Peer had arranged to have a three-man backing group on hand in the studio. Should Rodgers run short of material, the trio had some songs of their own.

The trio, named for this session The Three Southerners, were Joe Kaipo, a Hawaiian guitarist; Ellsworth T. Cozzens, a multi-instrumentalist of Hawaiian descent; and banjoist J. R. Ninde, of whom almost nothing is known. Cozzens was also a gifted songwriter and Rodgers liked two of his songs, *Dear Old Sunny South by the Sea* and *Treasures Untold.* Both songs were recorded with the trio backing Jimmie. *The Sailor's Plea,* a sentimental ballad, was the song Jimmie had selected from the batch sent to him by Elsie McWilliams. The final title cut on the 14th was *Brakeman's Blues.* This is usually considered to be accompanied by Jimmie's solo guitar, but the careful listener will detect a subtle ukulele backing, provided by Cozzens. The following day four more titles were cut, but these were more blues-orientated: *Memphis Yodel, Blue Yodel No. 2* and *In the Jailhouse Now* were the issued titles. This session is a minor landmark in Rodgers' career, for it was the first occasion that he was accompanied by a backing group. Rodgers was obviously intending to record solo, so the group must have been Peer's idea. How much influence Peer actually exercised on Jimmie's style and choice of material is not easy to ascertain, but one must assume that it was considerable.

Charles K. Wolfe has begun research on this interesting aspect and his work is invaluable here. Certainly Peer had pointed out to Rodgers, right from the first recordings, that original material was more profitable; and it does seem as if he was more interested in previously unrecorded songs. As Wolfe has put it:

> Did he [Peer] at that time somewhat equate 'original' compositions with folk songs? Or was he simply unaware of folk songs as such . . . Or did Peer already foresee the founding of his music publishing company?[3]

Obviously Peer had more to gain financially from original compositions; and certainly Victor would profit, for people were more likely to buy previously unrecorded songs. Fortunately, Peer has left some indication of the influence that he wielded at this particular session in his 1953 article:

> We worked hard far into the night getting enough material in shape for the first recording session. Actually, we did not have enough material, and I decided to use some of his blues songs to 'fill in'. When we recorded the first blues ('T for Texas') I had to supply a title, and the name "Blue Yodel" came out. The other Blue Yodels made at the same time had titles suggested by the words, but when I witnessed the tremendous demand for the original, I decided to change these names to "Blue Yodel No. 2", "Blue Yodel No. 3", etc.[4]

Peer, it would seem, had considerable influence in this instance at least.

There is one interesting comparison to be made here with Rodgers' second session. Mike Auldridge, the Washington, D.C., dobro-player and E. T. Cozzens' nephew, has reported that Cozzens was paid a flat fee of $40 for *Dear Old Sunny South*[5]: a reward notably worse than Kelly Harrell's for *Away Out on the Mountain*. Rodgers appears as co-writer of *Sunny South*, even though he could only have been the arranger.

Shortly after Jimmie's return to Washington, at the beginning of March, he received his second royalty cheque: this time for $400. This obviously made a considerable difference to their financial position and Carrie began to feel less worried, though she continued her job in the tearoom. They did indulge themselves with another, newer, second-hand Dodge. Jimmie was finding more work now that his records were selling, but his main problem was the search for suitable recording material.

Carrie frequently mentions that Jimmie continually had ideas for songs, writing down odd lines or snappy titles as they occurred to him. But now, in early 1928, his inability to sit down and complete a song was causing problems. He was now discovering that

> For all his shrewd planning . . . he'd made one bad slip-up. He had somehow never gotten around to bringing all those 'dandies' in the back of his head to the front . . . he was forced to 'dig'; to appeal to others to dig — for old, out-dated numbers which he could bring to life again, re-vamp and make his own. But what he needed to do, of course, was work out his own 'dandies' — for the sake of the added royalties that would be his, as lyricist and composer.[6]

Jimmie was unable to read or write music and, although a talented performer with a keen ear for a catchy phrase or title, he desperately needed someone to help him arrange and notate his music, help out when he was stuck for a line and collaborate generally. The answer to this problem came in the shape of Elsie McWilliams, Carrie's sister and the family 'poetess'. Elsie had already sent Jimmie some reworked ballads, but now they needed her in person.

When Jimmie and Elsie had played together, back in Meridian in the early '20s, it was probably Elsie who had helped Jimmie to learn the then current popular songs which made up their repertoire. She was a talented musician and had a way with words, having written many songs and poems. Though married, with three children, she responded quickly when Jimmie and Carrie asked her to come to Washington.

> Jimmie then asked me to come to Washington and help him get eight songs ready for his next recording as he played strictly by ear and he knew he could do better by the tunes if I was near to see that he learned them correctly. We had the eight ready in time![7]

Carrie Rodgers has described Elsie's arrival a little more graphically:

> She scurried to Washington, bringing with her all the sweet, ancient ballads and quaint ditties she could find in the stacks and stacks of old, once popular, sheet music at mother's. Bringing too, some of her own little verses which, as a more than capable musician, she had set to music.[8]

Elsie McWilliams, Rodgers' collaborator on many of his songs, in later life. Right, sheet music of an early Rodgers recording.

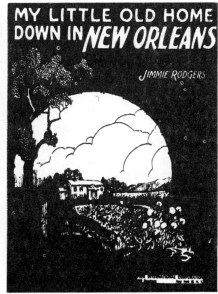

Jimmie and Elsie set to work to produce, or rearrange, songs for his next session. Carrie likened the activity to a 'music factory' working all hours of the day and night:

> Snatches of this and that; whang – twang – strum, some words – more words – repetition to drive a bystander mad![9]

But the Rodgers-McWilliams partnership was to be a profitable one in both musical and financial terms. Strangely, the Southern Music publications of these partnership songs invariably state: words by Elsie McWilliams, music by Jimmie Rodgers. Yet Rodgers could not read music and was, according to Carrie, the one who usually thought out the words; though it is quite probable that Jimmie had the tunes in his head and sang them while Elsie notated them. In an interview some years later with Jim Evans, Elsie claimed that she had helped with many more songs than had been copyrighted in her name and, in many cases, had written practically all the music and lyrics.[10] Unfortunately, Evans did not list these extra titles and we can only guess from the style the songs she may have helped to create without credit. In the Meridian *Star* article, Elsie did mention that

> I helped him with several of his blue yodels, but not many carried my name as we seldom agreed on points.[11]

Possibly, the disagreement may have arisen over the strong sexual references which Jimmie put into his blues material (discussed more fully in Chapter 7). For, after all, Elsie was the daughter of a churchman and a practising Christian.

But despite their close family relationship, Jimmie wanted the partnership with Elsie on a firm business footing. He insisted she must have a share of the royalties, and also that she should have a binding contract with Peer's Southern Music Company. This was finally accomplished in June 1928, when Elsie accompanied him to New York for his fourth recording session.

While working for WTFF, Jimmie made another valuable contact, Ray McCreath. McCreath was at that time WTFF's chief announcer, and he and Jimmie rapidly became close friends. According to Carrie Rodgers, it was McCreath who first used the title 'America's Blue Yodeler' to introduce Jimmie, a title which was to be used on most of his publicity material.[12] Because of his railroad association, Jimmie was often referred to as 'The Singing Brakeman' – occasionally both tags were used together. McCreath found engagements for Jimmie, and eventually resigned his job with WTFF to become his personal manager. How long this arrangement lasted is not easy to ascertain, but the relationship probably did not continue beyond late 1928. However, at the end of May, Jimmie, Elsie McWilliams and McCreath set out in the old Dodge for the short tour which the latter had arranged. Carrie Rodgers did not go with them, preferring instead to continue with her job in the tearoom. She felt if she left she might not get the job back; and living for so long on the bread line had made her extremely sceptical of Jimmie's apparent success in the world of show business.

Shortly after they had left, Carrie received a telegram from New York 'ordering' her to the city. Even though the cable was signed by Jimmie she feared that the excitement and hard work had brought on another haemorrhage. She rushed to New York with Anita and was met by Jimmie who explained that he had wanted to see 'his two', Carrie and Anita. He had arranged a visit to Coney Island for his family, but first they had to pick up the car. At the garage, Carrie waited impatiently for the old Dodge to be brought out, but Jimmie led her to a brand-new dark blue Buick, the car they had long ago decided they would most like to own. Carrie was naturally pleased, but reminded Jimmie that they had incurred many debts over the last few years, and that these now needed to be repaid. Jimmie had, in fact, already paid off some debts, but Carrie decided she would 'Keep working for ten years — for wages and tips — to help pay off those debts — just for the — for the knowing our dream would come true.'[13]

In June, Peer arranged another recording session: a lengthy one of twelve or so titles. Jimmie and Elsie had been working at full stretch to prepare material, and no problems were expected. As they were about to start for Camden, Elsie received a cable from her husband that Patricia, her eight-year-old daughter, was dangerously ill. Jimmie suggested that they should continue to Camden, and have telegrams sent to various places along the route informing them of Patricia's progress. If she was no better by the time they reached New York Elsie could catch an express straight to Meridian. This would seem to suggest that Jimmie was relying on Elsie to some considerable extent. Possibly he was not entirely happy with some of the new material, and wanted her close by in case he ran into difficulties. Fortunately, by the time they reached New York Patricia was out of danger. Elsie donated her first royalty cheque to the church in gratitude for her daughter's recovery. She stayed for the recording session, and then returned to Meridian.

This June recording session reveals an almost complete change in Rodgers' style and repertoire. The February recordings had all been heavily blues-orientated, but this next set of titles inclined to softer, more sentimental ballad material. All but one of the songs issued from the session were from the Rodgers-McWilliams partnership, and it must be to Elsie McWilliams' influence that the change should be attributed. *My Old Pal, Lullaby Yodel, You and My Old Guitar, Never No Mo' Blues, My Little Lady* and *Daddy and Home* were all big-selling titles. *Daddy and Home* had been written by Elsie while she was with Jimmie on tour, because he had spoken to her so much about his father. Only *My Little Lady,* a lively yodelling song, betrays any relationship to the earlier recordings, and the rakish tribute to 'Sadie' is almost totally out of keeping with the mood of the session. Compare for example:

I'm thinking of you tonight, old pal,
And wishing you were here,
I'm dreaming of the time in days gone by
When you filled my heart with cheer.
I remember the nights when all alone
We sang 'Sweet Adeline',
No other face can take the place
In my heart, old pal of mine.

(*My Old Pal*, Victor 21757)

and

I am dreaming tonight of an old southern town
and the best friend I ever had,
For I've grown so weary of roaming around
I'm going home to my dad.

(*Daddy and Home*, Victor 21757)

with material from the previous session, such as:

You can blow your whistle, Mama, you can toot your horn,
You're gonna wake up some morning and find your daddy gone.

(*Blue Yodel No. 2*, Victor 21291)

or

I woke up this morning, the blues all round my bed,
I didn't have nobody to hold my aching head.

(*Memphis Yodel*, Victor 21636)

However, all the titles from this session used only Jimmie's guitar as accompaniment. Only *My Little Old Home Down in New Orleans* did not come from the Rodgers-McWilliams partnership, and this, rather surprisingly, was the least popular of the songs issued from this session.

*　　*　　*

While at Victor, Jimmie had made the acquaintance of another of the company's top-selling artists, Gene Austin. Austin was then a popular crooner whose big hit had recently been *My Blue Heaven*; his real name was Gene Lucas and he began his career as a songwriter. Early in 1924 he called in to the Vocalion studios in New York to promote some songs and Cliff Hess, the recording manager (himself a notable composer), told him that he was worried. A Knoxville firm had sent a young man to New York in the belief that he could make a series of hillbilly records that would be very successful. The man was George Reneau, 'The Blind Musician of the Smoky Mountains', and whilst his guitar and harmonica playing was good his voice did not record well and he lacked a sense of timing. Several singers had been tried as his vocal partner but they did not have the Southern style necessary for the type of recording. Austin was asked to try and he was chosen. The duet recorded ten sides early in April 1924 and a brief friendship arose. Austin did not receive label credit but Vocalion paid him $25 per side. In June 1924 Austin vocalised for Uncle Am Stuart, a 74-year-old fiddler, again receiving no label credit. It is thought that Austin played banjo accompaniment on as many as eight of Am Stuart's recordings at this time, but this has not been confirmed. In September 1924 Austin and Reneau cut eight sides for Edison as The Blue Ridge Duo and there ended Austin's brief but fruitful excursion into country music. Around mid-1924 he had recorded a vocal duet with Carson Robison but this was not a hillbilly song. Austin had a very pleasant tenor voice and his lazy style had a slightly nasal delivery, thus many of his 1924-28 recordings with guitar, ukulele and violin accompaniment are of more than just passing interest. However, unlike Vernon Dalhart, he did not make the change to country music, probably because of his huge pop success with *My Blue Heaven,* a self-penned item that is still sung and recorded by many popular performers almost half a century on.

However, Jimmie and Gene became close personal friends, with a healthy respect for each other's talents. The Rodgerses and the Austins took several holidays together and in July 1928 went cruising on the Potomac River in Austin's yacht 'Blue Heaven'. It was also Gene Austin who provided the opportunity for Jimmie's first appearance in a 'real' theatre. His advice was not to waste time playing at small picture houses, but to go for big, reputable theatres.[14] Austin was a close friend of the manager of the Earle Theatre, at that time the most important in Washington. Austin persuaded the manager to take Jimmie as a 'Special Added Attraction' for the first week in August.

Appearing in a large theatre, with all the attendant problems of lighting, scenery and props, had its effect on Jimmie, who had never before been in the exciting, bustling world of show business. But Jimmie, with his customary down-to-earth manner, soon won over the backstage workers. At first they kidded him, asking what props he would need, what scenery, and so on. Finally, when the lighting engineer asked if he wanted 'spots' or 'foots', Jimmie replied, 'You can just gimme a coal oil lamp son, that'll do'.[15] Jimmie made his first performance in his blue brakeman's uniform, complete with peaked cap. He took the centre of the stage, propped his foot on a chair, and sang. According to Carrie, his choice of material for that first evening included *T for Texas, Soldier's Sweetheart,* and for his encore his own reworking of the traditional ballad *Frankie and Johnny.* As Carrie noted, 'In those days you didn't sing "Frankie and Johnny" in polite company nor in public to a mixed audience.'[16] But Jimmie did; and the audience loved it. He took 16 curtain calls that first evening, and Jack Pepper, the Earle's no doubt worried manager, was delighted. But the performance took its toll and after coming off stage Jimmie was on the point of collapse. In fact, only a stiff measure of whiskey had given him the strength to perform in the first place. Whiskey was the one prop that Jimmie couldn't do without. Carrie has suggested that Jimmie always had a couple of stiff drinks before a performance or a recording session on advice from his doctor. A drink helped keep his voice clear and prevented it breaking in the middle of a song. But drink was not just medicinal, for Jimmie, like many musicians, had a weakness for it.

The summer of 1928 could be said to be the time that Jimmie 'made it'. The record of *Blue Yodel* and *Away Out On The Mountain* had recently been released and was proving a mild sensation. The reviews of this record are most interesting. One piece, dated July 1928, reviews a Rabbit Brown recording (Brown was a black New Orleans singer) and then says: 'Meet also Jimmie Rodgers singing "Down on the Mountain" and his engaging, melodious and bloodthirsty "Blue Yodel" '.[17] It would almost seem as if the reviewer wasn't sure on which side of the colour line Jimmie stood. A September review makes it a little clearer:

> WHITE MAN SINGING BLACK SONGS. Part 2 of Jimmie Rodgers 'Blue Yodel', which started the whole epidemic of yodelling blues which now rages.[18]

A November review was more critical:

> WHITE MAN GONE BLACK. 'Blue Yodel No. 3' and 'Never No Mo Blues', Victor, sung by Jimmie Rodgers, whose singing and guitaring are as easy and as lazy as ever, but who needs a gag writer, for he is running short of gags.[19]

The review was correct when it spoke of an 'epidemic' of blue yodellers, for in the summer of 1928 the cover versions of Jimmie's records began to appear. Probably the first copy was by Frankie Marvin, who together with his brother Johnny was a familiar figure around the New York recording studios. The Marvins recorded widely and under a variety of labels — popular, novelty, sentimental and, of course, hillbilly. Frankie's cover version of *Blue Yodel* and *Away Out on the Mountain* appeared on Brunswick some time that summer. Interestingly, it was in the popular series (3979). Shortly after this, a coupling of *Blue Yodel No. 2* and *In*

The Jailhouse Now was released in the hillbilly series (Brunswick 249). Marvin performed the songs with yodel and simple guitar backing, the only difference being his use of a resonator guitar played with a steel bar. Probably Frankie was known to Jimmie, for certainly his older brother Johnny was a personal friend of the brakeman. Around the end of the year, Frankie Marvin recorded *Ben Dewberry* and *Mother Was A Lady*, which completed his cover versions of the recordings made at Jimmie's November 1927 session. About the same time Riley Puckett, Columbia's top-selling country vocalist, put out Jimmie's *Blue Yodel*. Although this was recorded in April 1928, we assume it was released after Marvin's initial copy.

But Jimmie's records were selling, especially in his beloved South, and Victor were advertising him widely; Carrie recalled seeing an advertisement for his records in a Washington bus as early as June.[20] People were taking notice of the Blue Yodeler, but in order to keep his name before the public he needed to tour, making personal appearances throughout the South. And this gruelling sort of performing was never easy, especially for a man suffering from severe tuberculosis. However, Jimmie was now a celebrity, and as Carrie later wrote,

> Everybody wanted to know about him. There was so little that anybody really did know. So – in no time at all – 'Everybody' knew so much about him that wasn't so, that never had been so, and that was never to become so.[21]

The Jimmie Rodgers legend was being born: from the mouths of journalists and the over-worked imaginations of radio announcers, a whole mythology began to emerge about the 'Singing Brakeman'. Suddenly, everyone knew something about him – and if it wasn't strictly true, nobody cared much; it was all good, folksy stuff. His first record had been issued in England in September 1928 (Zonophone 5158, *Blue Yodel/Away*

Out on the Mountain) but still less was known about him there. Even as late as 1935, two years after his death, the English Zonophone Company wrote:

> His life is a mystery, nothing definite is known about him; rumour reports him dead, but it just as strongly reports him as living.[22]

In the summer of 1928, before setting out on his first tour, Jimmie acquired some new instruments. He felt that his old guitar was not satisfactory for a show-business personality. Mrs Rodgers recalled that Gibson, Martin and Weymann, the leading instrument makers at that time, all 'vied with each other' to persuade him to use one of their models. Certainly he liked them all, and for his stage appearances he agreed to use the Weymann 'Jimmie Rodgers Special', a gold-inlaid $1500 instrument.

This had his name inlaid down the neck. When he had finished his act and was taking his bow, he would reverse the guitar and there on the back was 'Thanks', inlaid in mother-of-pearl.[23] This was Jimmie's stage instrument, but on his recordings he preferred to use a Martin. He had several that had his name inlaid down the neck. He also had at least two Gibson guitars, and a banjo and mandolin made by that company. His ukulele was almost certainly made by Martin.

In the early autumn, he set out on the first of his three tours of major circuits throughout the South and Southeast. This had probably been arranged by Ray McCreath, though doubtless Ralph Peer had had a hand in its organisation. The tour was to continue until December, and the principal theatres that Jimmie was to play in were on the Loew circuit, a theatre chain which had long used and promoted country music. Working his way south, Jimmie eventually reached Florida. It was here, perhaps, at this time that he performed before the 1600 members of the Men's Bible Class at their Sunday morning gathering. This booking at first worried Jimmie as he didn't know any 'church songs', but he was told to sing anything and complied with *In the Jailhouse Now,* to the great enjoyment of his audience. From Florida he headed north, to Atlanta, Georgia, where Ralph Peer had arranged a brief October recording session.

For the titles cut in Atlanta, Peer decided to experiment with various backings and made up a scratch group of studio musicians. Steel guitar,

Rodgers playing (left) *and advertising* (below) *the Special Model Weymann built for him in 1928. The advert dates from April 1930.*

trumpet, clarinet and string bass are all evident on the recordings. The overall effect of the backing on *Waiting for a Train, My Carolina Sunshine Girl, I'm Lonely and Blue* and *Blue Yodel No. 4 (California Blues)* is jazz-influenced. Pleasant though some of the sounds are, it seems amazing that Peer, who in 1927 had thought that the Tenneva Ramblers were 'incongruous' as Rodgers' backing, should now believe this motley group to be suitable. What kind of connection could there be between these recordings and folksong, the type of music Peer had once been so anxious to record? The answer seems to be that Peer was concerned with producing top-selling records. Jimmie Rodgers had a following with hillbilly record buyers, and now with a jazz backing Peer hoped his records would sell to the jazz-buying public. Throughout his recording career, Jimmie Rodgers was to be saddled with peculiar and often totally unsuitable backing groups. Ralph Peer himself has claimed the responsibility for this:

> The principal idea was to provide Jimmie with variegated accompaniments so that he would have as many different backgrounds as possible.[24]

In all fairness, two points should be noted here. First, Jimmie himself never made any complaint about the various backings Peer provided; he too was concerned with selling records. And secondly, it was almost certainly the wide-ranging accompaniments that made Jimmie's records so popular with others than country music fans. A country enthusiast might object to the backing, but would still buy the records, for nothing, even the most incongruous accompaniment, could mar the essential sound of Rodgers on record.

After recording Jimmie on 20 and 22 October, Peer returned to Bristol for another highly productive session. Arriving on 26 October, he was again interviewed by the *Herald-Courier.* The article mentioned Jimmie Rodgers and his considerable success:

> Referring to one of the characters which he ran into last year, Mr Peer said that Jimmie Rogers [*sic*] . . . an exceptional singer and yodeler . . . combined these two and produced his first record the 'Blue Yodel'.
>
> Later when the record was published the public went wild over the piece, and Jimmie was called to the factory to work regularly for the company. Now he is drawing over $15,000 a year, and is on a circuit booked for twelve weeks, making over a thousand a week. He produces a record every month for the Victor Company and is Gene Austin's keenest rival.[25]

Peer, of course, was mistaken in claiming that Jimmie's first record was *Blue Yodel,* but probably meant first hit. It seems likely that Peer used this article as another free advertisement for new talent; and one would imagine that Rodgers' success story would be a considerable spur to many young singers.

November 1928 was election month. The presidential candidates for that year were the Republican Herbert Hoover and the flamboyant Democrat Al Smith. Smith, a Roman Catholic, and a 'wet', didn't have a chance, even though he had been a highly successful governor of New York. Hoover won the election hands down with his message 'A chicken in every pot and two cars in every garage'. Seven months later came the worst economic depression that America had ever known. The interesting point here, however, is that while many country musicians were proclaiming their politics loud and strong, Jimmie Rodgers was amazingly silent for one of his background and upbringing. Uncle Dave Macon, 'The Dixie

Dewdrop', loudly declared,

> Al Smith nominated for president, my darling,
> My vote to him I'm gonna present, my darling.
>
> (*Governor Al Smith*, Brunswick 263)

And the following year was even to add a verse to one of his songs, consoling Al Smith on his defeat:

> Herbert Hoover was elected, Al Smith was rejected,
> But he's mighty well respected round Nashville.
>
> (*Uncle Dave's Travels Part 3*, Brunswick 355)

Country music has often been a political ally — one thinks of Jimmie Davis using his songwriting achievements to boost himself into the governorship of Louisiana; of the Leake County Revelers campaigning for Huey Long, and of a host of singers and musicians who played a part in political campaigns and elections. Yet Jimmie Rodgers recorded nothing of a political or socially controversial nature; hardly even a reference to the Depression, a subject that occurred in thousands of post-1929 songs. Rodgers seems, despite his background and railroad connections, to have been strangely apolitical. Whether this was really the case, or it was Ralph Peer who barred Jimmie from recording songs of a controversial nature, will never be known. But it is perhaps significant that his recording of *Prohibition Done Me Wrong* was his only title that was destroyed at the master stage. Rodgers was by no means unique in his avoidance of political or topical material, yet in this respect he seems more allied to the popular singers' camp than to the hillbilly school, where topical and social comment songs formed a significant percentage of the recorded repertoire.

However, as Ralph Peer left Atlanta for Bristol, so Rodgers headed south for Geiger, Alabama, where his father and second step-mother were living. As Carrie later wrote,

> All Geiger, was, of course, excited and delighted. The same old Jimmie! As tickled as ever to sit hunched on somebody's back porch whanging at a borrowed banjo, uke or mandolin.[26]

Jimmie spent much of his time in Geiger looking up old friends and visiting again the places he had known as a child. He and his father, despite their long separations, had always been close, and now Jimmie persuaded him to join the tour for a while. At some theatres he even had his father on stage with him. But the harsh conditions of touring, the one-night stands, the noisy hotel rooms, the managers and reporters, were taking their toll on his health. Whenever possible, Jimmie avoided hotels and booked in at tourist courts or rented cottages where he could rest without interruption. Fortunately, his first tour ended in December and he and Carrie spent Christmas at her parents' home in Meridian. But even here, when Jimmie was not working 'officially', he was usually to be found playing with, or for, old friends, or slipping away to entertain patients at local hospitals.

After finishing the tour, Jimmie had signed a contract with the Paul English Players, a tent show from Mobile, Alabama. Tent shows, according to Ralph Peer, were Jimmie's favourite venues, for he enjoyed the relaxed informality that was not to be found in 'real' theatres. According to Malone, featuring a 'name attraction' in a tent show for a limited engagement was considered something new; but Rodgers' appearances apparently doubled the show's takings.[27] The tour ranged from Mobile to Texas, where Jimmie's engagement ended in March 1929. He worked only as a concert feature, doing a 20-minute act each evening at a salary of $600 a week. The show had tie-ups with the Victor dealers in the local towns they played, and his recordings were offered for sale after each performance. It would be impossible to estimate how profitable this was, or how it affected his record sales, but there is every reason to suppose that it was highly successful. But even working for 20 minutes each night was a tremendous strain on Jimmie, and on several occasions he was too ill to appear.

In February 1929, the English Players arrived in Jimmie's home town, Meridian. Possibly the excitement of appearing in his own 'backyard' and the cumulative effect of touring almost non-stop since the previous September proved too much. Jimmie collapsed and was forced to miss several performances, much against his will. His place was taken by a 17-year-old Western Union messenger boy, Bill Bruner. Bruner had modelled his singing style on Jimmie and was a well-known performer around Meridian, often nicknamed 'The Singing Messenger Boy' or 'The Singing Salesman'. On 8 February, Bruner arrived at the theatre to watch the performance when Paul English came hurriedly from behind the curtain and walked straight up to him.

RODGERS, JIMMIE—America's Blue Yodler

Jimmie Rodgers

Title	Catalog		Title	Catalog
Away Out On the Mountain	21142			
Ben Dewberry's Final Run	21245			
Blue Yodel	21142			
Blue Yodel No. 2	21291			
Blue Yodel No. 3	21531			
Blue Yodel No. 4	V-40014			
Blue Yodel No. 5	22072			
Blue Yodel No. 6	22271			
Brakeman's Blues	21291			
Daddy and Home	21757			
Dear Old Sunny South by Sea	21574			
Desert Blues	V-40096			
Drunkard's Child	22319			
Everybody Does It in Hawaii	22143			
Frankie and Johnny	22143			
I'm Lonely and Blue	V-40054			
I'm Sorry We Met	22072	Never No Mo' Blues	21531
In the Jailhouse Now	21245	Sailor's Plea	V-40054
Jimmie's Texas Blues	22379	Sleep, Baby, Sleep	20864
Lullaby Yodel	21636	Soldier's Sweetheart	20864
Memphis Yodel	21636	Train Whistle Blues	22379
Mother Was a Lady	21433	Treasures Untold	21433
My Carolina Sunshine Girl	V-40096	Tuck Away My Blues	22220
My Little Lady	V-40072	Waiting for a Train	V-40014
My Little Old Home	21574	Whisper Your Mother's Name	22319
My Old Pal	21757	Yodeling Cowboy	22271
My Rough and Rowdy Ways	22220	You and My Old Guitar	V-40072

'Bill' he said, 'Jimmie's sick and can't go on. They tell me you sing like him. Come on.'[28]

Bill went. His opening number was Jimmie's favourite *Frankie and Johnny*. Bruner had to take six encores before the audience let him go. The next night he was called backstage to meet Jimmie, who gave him $10 and one of the first guitars he'd ever owned. (This is generally thought to be the Martin with which Jimmie made his first record.) Bruner kept the

Bill Bruner – left, *in 1929, and* right, *in 1953, with the guitar Rodgers gave him.*

guitar until 1953, when he presented it to Jimmie Rodgers Snow (see Chapter 7). After this initial performance, Bruner played several engagements with Jimmie and probably accompanied him on his tour with Swain's Follies in 1931. It seems likely that he stood in for Rodgers on other occasions when the latter was too ill to perform; but he had little ambition to be a professional performer and, despite his stage appearances and a handful of recordings on Okeh, soon retired from music.[29]

Towards the middle of February, Jimmie had recovered sufficiently to continue the tour. On the 21st he recorded in Dallas, Texas. Two titles were cut on that day and three on 23 February. *Desert Blues,* a bizarre but amusing song, suffered from its peculiar accompaniment of cornet, saxophone, tuba, violin, bass and percussion. *Any Old Time* suffers the same fate. However, the session of the 23rd was a different matter; *High Powered Mama* and *Blue Yodel No. 5* were good, straight blues, unadorned except for Jimmie's guitar; and a pleasant sentimental ballad, *I'm Sorry We Met,* came from the Rodgers-McWilliams partnership.

Jimmie was now a minor sensation with his records and personal appearances. Wherever he played he drew big crowds and, it would seem,

never faced a hostile audience. By all accounts he had a considerable stage presence and being a born showman, knew exactly how to use an audience. The following account by Malone describes this:

> Although he recorded with a diverse assortment of instrumental accompaniment ... his personal appearances were almost always made in solo fashion, just Jimmie and his guitar. For his stage appearances he generally dressed in a white or tan light-weight suit and sported a jauntily cocked straw sailor hat ... He looked and acted the part of a young man-about-town out for an evening of pleasure. He would put his foot on a chair, cradle his guitar across his knee, and captivate his audiences with a selection of both rakish and sentimental tunes that generally consumed no more than twenty minutes. In a voice unmistakably Southern he kidded his audiences in a whimsical fashion.[30]

Jimmie was rapidly becoming a rich man, drawing $600 a week from Paul English and with royalty cheques amounting to as much as $2000, as well as fees for local radio broadcasts and royalties on his songs. Yet with all this new-found wealth, the Rodgerses still did not have their own home — something Carrie had wanted for a long, long time. When Jimmie ended his tour with English in March 1929 he and Carrie decided on a brief vacation, and rented a small cottage in Kerrville, in southern Texas. Carrie realised that Texas would be an ideal location for their home. Meridian's moist climate could prove fatal to Jimmie's health; Washington suffered the harsh Northern winters; California was too far from the scene of his musical activities. Kerrville, however, seemed totally suitable, with its high altitude, dry air and warm, mild winters. It was still some distance from his working area, but not as far as California. Best of all, Kerrville was the site of one of the biggest government hospitals for tubercular ex-servicemen, and there Jimmie could have treatment.

Unable to buy any suitable accommodation, Jimmie purchased, in May, a plot of land in Westland Hills, just outside Kerrville, and decided to build his house there. The following months were an exciting time, planning and designing Jimmie's 'shanty'. The house was finished just in time for Christmas 1929, at a cost of approximately $50,000. While waiting its completion, Jimmie had thought of a name for it; as he explained to Carrie,

> Mother — know what? If you don't mind, I'd — sorta like to call it — Blue Yodeler's Paradise. Think that'd be okay?[31]

Carrie agreed, for it really did seem as if it was the house that the Blue Yodels had built.

Jimmie had a great love for Texas. It was there, according to Carrie, that he first 'flung out' his yodels, and it was there that he was to spend the remainder of his life: first in Kerrville and then in San Antonio. *T for Texas* was Jimmie's first big hit, and later, when he was made an honorary

Texas Ranger, he composed *Yodeling Ranger,* a song in tribute to that law-keeping force. He also recorded *Jimmie's Texas Blues,* perhaps one of his best songs; and in *Waiting for a Train* sang:

He put me off in Texas, a state I dearly love.

These Texas references were sufficient for many to assume erroneously that Jimmie was a Texan. But certainly the years that Jimmie spent in Texas were mainly happy ones.

On 8 and 10 August 1929, Jimmie recorded five titles in Dallas. These sessions mark another change in his musical direction. On *Everybody Does It in Hawaii* he was accompanied by the Burke Brothers — Billy on guitar and Weldon on ukulele — and Joe Kaipo on steel guitar. The piece is unmistakably pop-orientated and aimed at Hawaiian fans. *Tuck Away My Lonesome Blues* featured the same line-up with Bob McGimsey, the 'World's Greatest Whistler'. Even stranger things were to follow. On the 12th Jimmie recorded three takes of *Home Call,* and on the first and second Peer arranged for one L. D. Dyke to play musical saw. With the introduction of whistling and musical saw, Rodgers had been subjected to almost every conceivable style of accompaniment — except a rural stringband, which seems strange when one considers how popular stringband music was at that time. However, other items from the session

Rodgers with (left to right) *Billy Burke, Weldon Burke and Joe Kaipo, accompanists in August 1929.*

were in the more usual white blues style. *Frankie and Johnny,* which he had long been featuring in his stage act, and *Train Whistle Blues* were perhaps the best products of the session. The remainder of 1929 was to be a busy time for Jimmie, and he was to record on three more occasions: in October in Dallas, and in November in New Orleans and Atlanta.

On 22 October, in Dallas, Jimmie recorded six songs. With a steel guitarist (probably Joe Kaipo) he sang *Whisper Your Mother's Name* and *My Rough and Rowdy Ways,* which has interesting autobiographical elements. With solo guitar, Jimmie recorded the sixth instalment in the *Blue Yodel* series, *Land of My Boyhood Dreams, Yodelling Cowboy* and *I've Ranged, I've Roamed, I've Travelled* — the four providing a good cross-section of his various styles: blues, sentimental ballads, and the rather unusual style of autobiographical song that Jimmie handled so well. At this Dallas session there is a break in the master numbers where the Burke Brothers recorded two titles while Jimmie was resting, and presumably, gaining strength to continue.

Probably in the same month Gene Autry, a young ex-railroad telegrapher from Oklahoma, began his recording career. Autry, destined to become an even bigger star than Rodgers and the hero of hundreds of B-Westerns, was heavily under Rodgers' influence at the onset of his recording career. It is possible that Autry's recording career began earlier than October 1929, for he produced several sides for the obscure Cova Company whose recordings were released on Grey Gull, Radiex, Van Dyke and Sunrise and are impossible to date with any degree of certainty. These Cova recordings were yodelling songs in the Rodgers style. However, in October Autry recorded for Victor.

His first recordings were a pair of duets with his partner Jimmie Long, the Marvin brothers, Johnny and Frankie, providing the accompaniment of two steel guitars. Frank Marvin also yodelled on this session. Johnny Marvin, the elder brother, had been a session-man and featured vocalist for many labels including Victor and had introduced Frankie to the recording life. Both Marvins were instrumental in persuading Victor to record Autry and Long. Apart from these two Victor sides most of Autry's recordings from 1929-33 were very much in the Rodgers style and his recorded repertoire included many Rodgers songs. His first copy of a Rodgers song was his 24 October 1929 recording for Columbia of *Blue Yodel No. 5.* His vocal style was extremely similar to Rodgers' and often his yodel was almost as good. His guitar-playing was a little stilted, particularly when he attempted to copy the Rodgers runs, but the overall sound can be described as a near-perfect copy.

With Autry's entry into the recording field, the Rodgers following was becoming a strong force. Another artist who had been strongly influenced by the Singing Brakeman was the Texan Jimmie Davis. Davis, later to enter politics and eventually to become Governor of Louisiana, was to win fame as a songwriter with his maudlin compositions *You Are My Sunshine* and

Nobody's Darling But Mine. His early records, however, were mainly white blues, very much in the Rodgers blue yodel style, except that Davis went further than Rodgers and certain of his blues titles contain very strong sexual references.

Jimmie was back in the studio again on 13 November, but for only one title. Here in New Orleans Jimmie recorded one of his most famous songs,

Left, *Gene Autry, who recorded many of Rodgers' songs like* Whisper Your Mother's Name. *"Luke Baldwin" was a* nom de disque *for Bill Cox.*

Hobo Bill's Last Ride. Perhaps more than any other of his songs, *Hobo Bill* combines the hobo and railroad themes in a highly successful, if somewhat sentimental, ballad. The song began life as a poem by fellow railroader Waldo O'Neal of New Mexico. Elsie McWilliams is supposed to have set the poem to music, but if she did she received no credit. Rodgers used only guitar and an occasional train whistle noise — made in the back of his throat — for accompaniment.

On the 25th Jimmie recorded again, this time in Atlanta; but the heavy pace of his schedule was beginning to tell, and four days were required to record only eight songs. With Jimmie at this session was Elsie, who had prepared material for the recordings, and Billy Burke, who was to accompany him on guitar. Elsie was credited with *Nobody Knows But Me*, the rather moralising *She Was Happy Till She Met You* and *Blue Yodel No. 7* (the only one of the *Blue Yodels* for which she received composer credit). *No. 7* is subtitled *Anniversary Blue Yodel*, because, as Victor's advertisement put it, 'it marks the third year during which this popular artist has been on the Victor roster'. The first *Blue Yodel* was recorded two Novembers previously, in 1927. Another peculiarity of this session was Jimmie's recording of what was to be *Blue Yodel No. 11*. The item — originally filed simply as *Blue Yodel* — was held over by Victor and eventually released in its correct place after *No. 10*. Presumably it was Peer or Victor who numbered the yodels and who decided that this should be *No. 11*; the methods of their selection are an interesting topic of speculation. Billy Burke plays second guitar on the issued takes.

Burke was also on some takes of other songs recorded at this session, but the released versions of *Mississippi River Blues, Nobody Knows But*

Me, A Drunkard's Child, That's Why I'm Blue and *Why Did You Give Me Your Love* are all solo guitar pieces, in which it is possible that Jimmie does not play at all, but limits himself to singing while Burke plays guitar. *A Drunkard's Child* had been written by Andrew Jenkins, composer of Jimmie's earlier hit *Ben Dewberry's Final Run*. Jenkins was a prolific hillbilly writer and usually specialised in disaster songs such as *The Death of Floyd Collins* and *Kinnie Wagner*.

It was not surprising that Jimmie was close to collapse at this session for the previous autumn had seen some hectic travelling. In September he had been in Camden, where he had made his first and only film, *The Singing Brakeman*. It was a Columbia-Victor 15-minute short, directed by Colonel Jasper F. Brady, and was made in Victor's studio, where a stage set had been constructed to resemble a railroad depot lunchroom. On the call-board on the wall, Jimmie had even written in the names of his old railroad friends: 'Martin, Strobel, Oliver and Harper – Engine 6977 – 10.15 am.' The two actresses, and the man who walks briefly across the set in the opening shot, are not credited in the cast list, and even Jimmie's name is listed as 'Jimmy Rogers'. The story-line, such as it is, has railroader Jimmie entering the lunchroom, presumably looking for a cup of coffee. The two women begin to discuss his singing and he is persuaded to perform for them. He delivers three songs, *T for Texas*, *Daddy and Home* and *Waiting for a Train*. Only the latter differs significantly from his previously recorded version, for here Jimmie uses only his guitar for accompaniment, and starts with a blast from his famous train whistle. According to Sydonia M. Young, C. F. Martin III personally delivered an inlaid Martin 000-45 guitar to Jimmie in Camden so that he could use it in the film.[32] The director apparently saw nothing incongruous in a blue-denimed brakeman in a tumble-down lunchroom playing a $1,500 guitar with his name emblazoned down the neck.

The film was advertised widely as an

> instrumental and vocal presentation that is unique in conception and clever in execution. It features Jimmy Rogers [*sic*], one of the cleverest guitar players on the professional stage.[33]

Details of the distribution of the film are by no means easy to ascertain, but Carrie does mention that her sister saw the film in a Washington theatre in early 1930.[34] But however widely the film may have been shown in the early 1930s, prints today are extremely rare.

1929 had been a successful year for Jimmie Rodgers. His recordings had topped the Victor best-sellers list, more and more offers of work were flooding in, and he was having his own spacious home built in Texas. But for millions of his fellow Americans, the autumn of that year was to see them facing personal disaster on an unprecedented scale. The economic boom following World War I ended abruptly in the Wall Street crash – the total collapse of the stock market, heralding the worst depression that

"THE SINGING BRAKEMAN"

THE CAST

Players	Characters
Jimmy Rogers	Jim

THE TECHNICAL STAFF

Directed by	Col. Jasper E. Brady
Cameramen	{Dal Clawson {Frank Zukor
Stage Settings by	Eddie Kahn
Recorded by	Sooy Brothers
	Western Electric System

THE STORY IN BRIEF

THE SINGING BRAKEMAN is an instrumental and vocal presentation that is unique in conception and clever in execution. It features Jimmy Rogers, one of the cleverest guitar players on the professional stage. He has won international reputation for his songs with human appeal.

Against the picturesque background of a railroad station, Jim, the singing brakeman, strums his songs while waiting for a cup of coffee. He has been called for the 10.15 train and takes a hasty bite at the waiting-room lunch. The counter girl is fond of Jim's selections and requests him to render "Waiting for the Train," "Dear Old Dad," and "T for Texas." The last is a humorous ditty of many verses, each funnier than the previous. The music of the three songs is catchy and before Rogers has finished his first number, he has his audience with him.

As a short subject, "The Singing Brakeman" stands in a class by itself. It will round out any program in any theatre anywhere. Old and young alike of both sexes will enjoy the melodious voice of Jimmy Rogers, who has sung his way to the hearts of millions. The atmosphere of the railroad station, the kindly woman behind the refreshment counter and the characterization of Rogers are full of romance and recall the happy hours spent in the country during a vacation period or in childhood days. This is the reason why "The Singing Brakeman" has proved so popular wherever it has been shown.

Still from, and trade handout for, The Singing Brakeman.

America had ever known. Not only were the giant corporations forced into liquidation, but millions of small investors and businessmen were wiped out. Shopkeepers and farmers were pushed out of business or off their land as banks across the continent foreclosed mortgages in a desperate effort to stay in business themselves. Millions of men began a fruitless search for non-existent jobs, tramping the country or jumping freight trains. No form of business was left untouched by the Great Depression,

Above, *Blue Yodeler's Paradise, the $50,000 home Rodgers had built in Kerrville, Texas, in 1929. In the* lower *picture are the family's black maid Anna and one of Rodgers' beloved cars.* Right, *some of the record hits that made it all possible, from a Victor catalogue of 1929.*

RODGERS, JIMMIE

JIMMIE RODGERS.

Born into a family of railroaders, at Meridian, Miss., Jimmie Rodgers, when little more than a child, went to work on the road as a common laborer. Curiously enough, the music which was to cause his rise to affluence, began simultaneously with his first employment. The old songs and ballads of the railroad, some born of pioneer toil on the railroads, some the crooning songs of the hoboes who were attracted to the new railroads like crows to a farmer's fence —these constituted the music that Jimmie Rodgers first knew. He learned to play the guitar, and to sing in a naturally appealing voice the songs of the road. Later Jimmie became a brakeman but his health failed. He wandered about the country, his guitar and his voice providing the necessities of life.

A Victor recording expedition into the mountains of Tennessee discovered Jimmie Rodgers, quite accidentally. From the first impromptu recording, Jimmie's Victor records have been tremendously successful. He is now a headline vaudeville artist, and his Victor success grows greater with each succeeding record.

RECORDS BY JIMMIE RODGERS

Away Out On the Mt.	21142	Desert Blues	V-40096	My Little Old Home	21574
Ben Dewberry's		I'm Lonely and		My Old Pal	21757
Final Run	21245	Blue	V-40054	Never No Mo' Blues	21531
Blue Yodel	21142	I'm Sorry We Met	22072	Sailor's Plea, The	V-40054
Blue Yodel—No. 2	21291	In the Jailhouse		Sleep Baby Sleep	20864
Blue Yodel—No. 3	21531	Now	21245	Soldier's Sweetheart	20864
Blue Yodel—No. 4	V-40014	Lullaby Yodel	21636	Treasures Untold	21433
Blue Yodel—No. 5	22072	Memphis Yodel	21636	Waiting for Train	V-40014
Brakeman's Blues	21291	Mother Was a Lady	21433		

and among the record companies many of the smaller concerns went out of business for ever, while the giants like Victor and Columbia were forced to cut down expenditure in every direction in a desperate bid to stay in production. Many fine hillbilly artists were dropped from the files by these companies and most returned to the obscurity of their rural homes and the mines or mills of the Southeastern states. Kelly Harrell, author of Jimmie's hit *Away Out on the Mountain,* was dropped by Victor because he was unable to play an instrument himself and Victor were not prepared to hire musicians to accompany him.[35] Yet, surprisingly, the Depression had little effect on the career of Jimmie Rodgers. In fact, the grim years 1930-2 saw him rise to even wider popularity and acclaim.

Just before Christmas 1929 the Rodgerses moved into their new home in Kerrville. Carrie hired a black girl, Anna, to help with the running of the big house. Jimmie was touring at the time of the move but he intended to be home for Christmas. On his return he cabled Carrie to meet him at the Sunset Station in San Antonio. For her present he gave her a brand new seven-seat Packard and a diamond brooch. The Christmas of 1929 was indeed a good one for Carrie and Jimmie Rodgers.

5 / The T.B. Blues

My good gal's trying to make a fool out of me
Trying to make me believe I ain't got that old T.B.

(T.B. Blues)

By January 1930 time was running out for Jimmie Rodgers. Living in the dry Texas climate at Kerrville did help, but the exhausting tours and personal appearances neutralised this benefit. Kerrville was a considerable distance from the centre of his musical activities, a long drive even from Dallas and San Antonio, where Victor had recording studios. As far as possible Peer helped by arranging recording sessions wherever Jimmie was, and thus reduced some of his travelling. Yet in order to maintain his position at the top of the hillbilly popularity tree, Rodgers needed to keep himself in the public eye by personal appearances and concert tours. Over the next two years, these appearances became more and more dependent upon the state of his health, and frequently had to be postponed or cancelled at short notice. Gradually, and despite the two wide-ranging tent-show tours Jimmie was to make, the area of his performances narrowed until by the end of 1932 it had become a small circle around the immediate vicinity of his Texas home.

In 1930, Jimmie's cough was growing worse and he began to lose weight alarmingly. Often he appeared on stage with a temperature so high that he was hardly aware of what he was doing. He refused to enter a sanatorium because of his many commitments, and probably because of the fear that he would never be able to leave again. Without doubt, Jimmie Rodgers was a man of great courage who fought his disease with fortitude, and held on to life with both hands; a man brave enough to mock the disease which was rapidly killing him, in songs such as the *T.B. Blues* and the cynical *Whippin' That Old T.B.* The only temporary relief from the grim reality of the disease was provided by alcohol — good 'sippin' whiskey'.

By implication, it is often suggested that Jimmie Rodgers was a drunk: an alcoholic even. This seems to be based mainly on his singing and the spoken comments on his records, where his voice sounds thick and slurred; but also on his legendary reputation as a 'hell-raiser'. However, it should be remembered that Rodgers had a strong southern accent with certain highly distinctive pronunciations, no doubt attributable, as Porterfield has suggested, to his early associations with the black railroad workers in his native Mississippi.[1] But a liberal dosing of whiskey mixed with honey before a performance or a recording take had been recommended by his doctor as helping to prevent his voice breaking and holding back his cough. There is little reason to suppose that Jimmie was an alcoholic. When Gid Tanner, the Georgia fiddler and leader of the well-known stringband the Skillet-Lickers, was interviewed shortly before his death in 1959, one question put to him was 'Would you call him [Rodgers] a drunk?' He replied:

> He was anyway you'd want him to be ... he'd stay sober ... and he'd stay drunk. When he got ready he'd go to drinking.[2]

Tanner often met Jimmie Rodgers in Atlanta and knew him well. Probably, when they met they would throw a party and drink too much — few musicians would not do the same. Alcohol would almost certainly have helped Jimmie to cope with the fact that his 'time wasn't long'. One assumes from Tanner's comments that Jimmie would set about some heavy drinking every now and then, and it was stories about these sessions that gave rise to the legend that he was an alcoholic. Moreover, during the whole Prohibition Era, which lasted until 1933, thousands of ordinary men and women, who had been only moderate drinkers before the Volstead Act, now suddenly found it necessary to consume vast amounts of illicit, often rot-gut, alcohol — perhaps to prove that they were not subject to a piece of unpopular legislation which a forceful minority had imposed upon the nation. As we noted earlier, the only master of Jimmie's which was destroyed before it could be issued was entitled *Prohibition Done Me Wrong.* One would assume that it was a song condoning moonshine. According to the Victor files the master was 'accidentally destroyed', but one is tempted to wonder if Ralph Peer thought the song might be harmful to Jimmie's image and thus decided not to issue it.

Even with his worsening condition, there was little change in Jimmie's personality. He remained the same high-spirited, happy-go-lucky character he had always been. 'Everybody was glad to see him, you know,' said Gid Tanner, testifying to Jimmie's popularity with friends and fellow

Clayton McMichen in the 1930s and, right, *Gid Tanner in 1922.*

musicians.[3] Clayton McMichen, who was associated with both Tanner and Rodgers, has also mentioned the latter's high spirits and generous nature:

> He was very high-strung. He'd play any kind of trick on you he could. A born jokester who didn't care about backstage Johnnies. If he saw someone he liked, he would give him fifty dollars, just like that.[4]

Carrie Rodgers confirms McMichen's statement about her husband's generosity. Having been poor for so long, it was natural that the Rodgerses should enjoy their new-found wealth, and as Carrie has said,

> It may be said of us that we kept cash in circulation – much of it in Texas – all through the Great Depression. If either of us saw something we longed to possess, we bought it without a second thought. We made loans too, casually and without security – lifting friends and mere acquaintances out of tight spots.[5]

Jimmie's earnings were high, but his generosity and extravagance – especially his passion for expensive cars – together with his mounting medical costs, meant that he needed to work, and work hard and often. So in March 1930 Jimmie began his second major tour, with the W. I. Swain Tent Show – 'The Hollywood Follies of 1930'.

The Follies were a typical touring show of the period and included such acts as an Irish comedian, a blues singer (one would like to know who) and

JIMMY RODGERS
- BORGER -
SUNDAY NIGHT
MAY 4
SWAIN'S
HOLLYWOOD FOL
AND
JIMMY RODGE
- BORGER
SUNDAY NIGHT
MAY
SWAIN'S
HOLLYWOOD FOL
AND
JIMMY RODGER
- BORGER -
SUNDAY NIGHT
MAY 4

a Hawaiian group, with Jimmie as the 'featured star attraction'. Bill Bruner was also present for at least several weeks of this tour. And it was Bruner who, once again, stepped in when Jimmie was too ill to perform. According to Malone, Jimmie was the 'outstanding hit of the show'.[6] The Follies toured through Louisiana, Mississippi and Texas drawing capacity crowds, and doing especially well in the Lone Star State. Malone's research, based upon contemporary *Billboard* reports, has suggested that once the show moved into Oklahoma and Kansas business fell off. The decline was eventually attributed to the fact that Jimmie was almost unknown in the area. Eventually he was replaced by the silent film comedian Ben Turpin.[7] This seems a reasonable explanation if one accepts the traditional view that Rodgers, at this time, was almost unknown outside the South. However, as we hope to show later, this statement has been greatly exaggerated. Jimmie was less well known, perhaps, above the Mason-Dixon Line, but certainly this could not have affected his crowd-pulling ability, for he was sufficiently celebrated in the Midwest to draw good audiences.

In a letter Jimmie wrote to Ralph Peer, dated 8 October 1930, there is a curious sentence:

> . . . A letter from Mdn. Miss. today telling me W. I. Swain is going to sue me for fifty grand. But I ain't a Dam bit afraid of that.[8]

Now this seems to suggest that, contrary to the *Billboard* report, Jimmie had left Swain without being replaced. Bill Bruner has stated that Jimmie left the show because of ill-health.[9] In view of the lack of further evidence, we can only speculate what really happened. But perhaps Jimmie, troubled by illness, took offence at Swain's suggestion that it was his fault that the show wasn't doing too well in the Midwest, and left claiming he was too ill to work. This would give Swain the idea that he had grounds for suing Jimmie for breach of contract; but whatever the reason, Swain's threat to sue never materialised. However, the spring and summer of 1930 was certainly a period of consistent illness for the Singing Brakeman.

During the middle of March, Jimmie was booked to appear at three evening concerts at the Fox Theatre in the small town of Carthage, Mississippi.[10] His appearances were the subject of a lead story in the local newspaper, *The Carthaginian.* The theatre owner, George Chadwick, paid Jimmie $500 a night for the concerts. Admission was one dollar — about two days' wages for a labouring man at that time. Rodgers was extremely ill during the time of his visit to Carthage and could only play for a short time each evening. During the afternoon of the first concert, on Thursday, 13 March, Rodgers heard a local stringband rehearsing in the hotel in which he was staying and invited them to his room for drinks. He explained his problem to them — that he was not able to play for more than 20 minutes or so — and asked for their help, which they were eager to

THE CARTHAGINIAN

VOLUME 59   CARTHAGE, LEAKE COUNTY, MISS., 'SIPPI, MARCH 13, 1930   NO. 1

Jimmie Rodgers in Person Is Here, At The Carthage Theatre, Thursday, Friday, Sat'day, Mar. 13, 14, 15--World's Famous Blue Yodler

give. The band (later to record for Okeh as Freeny's Barn Dance Band) was a fairly typical stringband outfit of two fiddles and guitar.

The Thursday and Friday shows were completely sold out — yet another example of Rodgers' popularity, considering the high price of admission and the fact that this was during the worst time of the Depression. At the concerts the local trio played several tunes with Jimmie vocalising, and then a couple more with him sitting in on guitar. Rodgers then did his solo spot for as long as possible and finally called back the trio to relieve him and to finish the evening. Hubert Cannon, son of Fonzo Cannon, the guitarist in the Carthage band, was in the audience, and recalls that Jimmie was pale and tired throughout his visit. On the Saturday morning Jimmie had a serious haemorrhage and a local doctor ordered him to remain in bed. The evening show had to be cancelled, Chadwick refunded the ticket money, and Jimmie in turn returned his fee to the theatre manager. The trio were not paid for their performances but all of them considered it a great honour to be on the same bill as the Blue Yodeler. Hubert Cannon later wrote,

> My father told me that Jimmie was very grateful and just kept telling them how much they had helped him. My father always thought of him as a fine gentleman and a common man even though he was very famous at this time.[11]

The split with Swain's tent show probably occurred about the end of June. As this happened in the Midwest, Ralph Peer arranged Jimmie's next recording session for July in Los Angeles, probably feeling that it would be less tiring for Jimmie than returning to Atlanta, New York or Texas. Jimmie probably wanted to visit the movie capital, too, and looked upon the trip as a working holiday; certainly the California sun would be of benefit to his health. He and Carrie arrived in Los Angeles about 28 June. The recording session was to be a long-drawn-out affair lasting from 30 June until 17 July. Jimmie recorded a total of 14 songs, all amazingly varied in style and mood. The long duration of the California session was no doubt in order to give the singer plenty of time to see all the sights and meet some of the film world's celebrities.

On 30 June Jimmie recorded *My Blue Eyed Jane,* written by Elsie McWilliams' niece Lulu Belle White about her sister Ruth. The accompaniment for this song was provided by cornet, clarinet, tuba, piano, banjo and guitar, played by Bob Sawyer and his band. The overall sound is swinging and heavily jazz-influenced. The same lineup was used on the Waldo O'Neal/Bob Sawyer composition *Jimmie's Mean Mama Blues,* a fine earthy song cut on 10 July. On the 16th Jimmie recorded *Blue Yodel No. 9 (Standin' On The Corner).* The Victor files are silent as to the accompanying musicians but it has been suggested that the cornet and piano on this record were played by Louis and Lil Armstrong respectively. For some time this has been a bone of contention among jazz experts but it now seems that most critics accept the jazzman's presence. As several of the other titles from this Californian session feature cornet, some authorities feel that Louis Armstrong was present on them too, but this is somewhat less probable, and we shall not commit ourselves to a definite statement. However, one thing is certain from the titles recorded at this session: Peer was providing Jimmie with every gimmick in the book to ensure that he always had something new to offer his public. Interestingly, *Blue Yodel No. 9* bears some similarity to the much recorded *Frankie and Johnny.*

> My good gal loves me, everybody knows,
> She paid a hundred dollars just for a suit of clothes.
>
> > (*Blue Yodel No. 9,* Victor 23580)
>
> Frankie was a good gal, as everybody knows,
> Spent a hundred dollars, just to buy her Johnny clothes.
>
> > (*Frankie And Johnny,* Victor 22143)

The girl in *No. 9* also comes looking for the singer, as Frankie does, with a '44 gun'.

Peer had asked Jimmie for a sequel to the popular *In The Jailhouse Now,* and on 12 July *In The Jailhouse Now No. 2* was duly recorded. This was cut with only Jimmie's guitar as accompaniment, as was *Pistol Packin' Papa,* one of Jimmie's more earthy numbers:

> Now girls I'm just a good guy, and I'm going to have my fun,
> And if you don't want to smell my smoke, don't monkey with my gun.
>
> > (*Pistol Packin' Papa,* Victor 22554)

Many of the remaining titles from the session feature an Hawaiian-style backing. This was provided by a well-known West Coast group, Lani McIntyre's Hawaiians, featuring Lani on guitar, with steel guitar, ukulele and string bass. The Victor files do not state that McIntyre's band were present on *Why Should I Be Lonely* and *I'm Lonesome Too,* but aural evidence would certainly seem to indicate their presence. Of all the strange accompaniments that Ralph Peer provided for Jimmie, perhaps this quartet are the best. They were all competent musicians who knew how to provide a subtle backing, and the steel guitar breaks are extremely good by any standard.

On the 17th Jimmie recorded a dialogue with I. N. Bronsen, of whom nothing is known. The master number comes from a special series allocated to West Coast recordings, and, as far as we have been able to ascertain, only a test was made. Entitled *The Pullman Porters,* the piece is a humorous sketch akin to Moran and Mack's then popular *Two Black Crows* routines. It opens with one of the characters whistling a snatch of blues, then 'Hiram' (Bronsen) calls on 'Hezekiah' (Rodgers) to read for him a telegram he has just received. Hezekiah informs him that he is the father of a new son. The news has to be repeated twice before it sinks in; then Hezekiah asks Hiram what his wife thinks of the happy event. 'Son,' says Hiram, 'that's what's troublin' me. She don't know nothin' about it.' Hiram then shows the roll of money he has won in a crap game, and Hezekiah promptly engages him in a change-giving routine which leaves Hiram six dollars poorer. Hiram has just pointed this out when the recording finishes.

Jimmie and Carrie also had the opportunity to meet the famous movie comedians Stan Laurel and Oliver Hardy, and were entertained to lunch by producer Hal Roach. But following the haemorrhage in March and the exhausting tour with Swain's tent show, Jimmie was close to collapse. The Rodgerses returned to Kerrville where Jimmie was ordered to take a complete rest. He performed little for the remainder of the year but refused to remain in bed like an invalid. Jimmie may not have been able to travel any distance, but there was plenty to keep him busy in Texas. In September he was in Galveston, and in October in Houston, making personal appearances and once even judging a beauty contest. He spent much of his time preparing new material for his next recording session, and relaxing by hunting in the hills around Kerrville with close friends. By now his medical costs were mounting rapidly and he had to employ a private nurse; a doctor had to be kept in attendance. These heavy expenses meant that Jimmie could not afford to remain idle for very long.

The summer and autumn of 1930 had seen severe hardship in Texas, Arkansas and Oklahoma, for, as well as the general effects of the Depression, the area had been hard hit by a serious drought. This was followed by a severe winter and drastic flooding of the Red River. Jimmie and Carrie had kept pace with the news of these disasters and by Christmas 1930 Jimmie was planning something concrete to help victims of the floods. At first he considered a concert tour throughout the region donating all the profits to relief agencies for the homeless and the destitute. Then, over the radio, he heard that Will Rogers, the homespun, crackerbarrel humorist and philosopher, had already planned a series of benefit concerts in northeast Texas for the relief of flood victims.[12] The tour had been jointly sponsored by the Red Cross and the Texas financiers Amon G. Carter, Jesse Jones and Houston Harte. Jimmie had long been an admirer of Rogers (and had been most disappointed not to have met him during his recent trip to California), and decided to offer his services. He sent the following cable to Rogers:

> If you have any room for me on your program I gladly offer my
> services, not only here but any place.[13]

His offer was gratefully accepted by the tour organisers and Jimmie invited
Will Rogers to accept the hospitality of Yodeler's Paradise for the duration
of his stay in Texas.

Towards the end of January 1931 Will Rogers flew down to San
Antonio, and on the 26th the tour opened at the Crystal Ballroom. In
addition to Will and Jimmie, the bill included Chester Byers and a group
Carrie Rodgers calls the 'Revelers'. (Could this have been the fine
Mississippi string band the Leake County Revelers?) The show was
attended by a considerable number of leading Texans and a substantial
sum of money was raised. On stage, Will introduced Jimmie as 'my distant
son' and Jimmie carried on the joke by calling Will 'dad'.[14] That night,
Will returned with Jimmie to Kerrville. Entering Rodgers' 'shanty' he dryly
asked 'Well, Jimmie, make all this with your throat?'[15]

The following day, after reporters had interviewed and photographed
them, they left for San Angelo and another concert. Here they were to
meet the famous aviator Frank Hawkes, who was to transport the party in
his plane 'The Hell Diver'. However, torrential rain had turned Wilburn

Below, *Rodgers with aviator Frank Hawkes and Will Rogers, Fort Worth,
Texas, 1931, while on the Red Cross benefit tour.* Right, *Rodgers and
Rogers outside Yodeler's Paradise.*

Field into a marshland and the San Angelo flight had to be cancelled. The party were determined to reach their destination and set off on the 300-mile drive in Carrie's Packard and another borrowed car, arriving in time for the performance. Throughout the spring, Jimmie and Will Rogers made benefit appearances in aid of Depression victims. Jimmie's friendship with the humorist meant a great deal to him and, as Carrie recalled, one of his favourite photographs was of the two of them standing outside Jimmie's Kerrville home.

At the end of January, Jimmie found time to record at the Texas Hotel in San Antonio. Although only three songs were cut on the 31st, two of them are among his most significant recordings. Sometime before this session, Jimmie had met Shelly Lee Alley, a young stringband musician. Shelly had written several songs for the yodeller and at this session Jimmie recorded one of them, *Travellin' Blues*. Appropriately, it was Shelly's stringband that provided the accompaniment. The record demonstrates some excellent guitar work by Charles Kama, a musician Jimmie was to use again. But it is the other two songs from this session that we consider important. *Jimmie the Kid*, co-written by Jack Neville, is a revealing autobiographical song:

> I'll tell you a story of Jimmie the kid
> He's a brakeman you all know.
> He was born in Mississippi way down South,
> And he flagged on the T. and N.O.

The song continues to list all the railroads that the brakeman had worked for, and eventually tells of his success. With obvious pride and great pleasure, Jimmie sings:

> He's got a beautiful home all of his own,
> It's the Yodeler's Paradise.

(Jimmie the Kid, Victor 23549)

The second song was *T.B. Blues,* a song which reveals a stoical attitude to the disease that was rapidly killing him. In many ways, Jimmie makes light of his illness and takes a fatalistic attitude:

> My good gal's trying to make a fool out of me,
> Trying to make me believe I ain't got that old T.B.

Some of the lines graphically describe the disease —

> My body rattles like a train on that old S.P.

— and it ends on a fatalistic note:

I've been fighting like a lion, looks like I'm going to lose,
Cause there ain't nobody ever whipped the T.B. blues.

(T.B. Blues, Victor 23535)

Tuberculosis — consumption — was a common, almost endemic disease amongst Southern blacks living in a damp, unhealthy climate, or in the crowded, insanitary shanty towns; and even among the inhabitants of the crumbling and overpopulated Northern ghettos. Several TB blues had been recorded by black singers prior to Jimmie's recording. Willie Jackson recorded his *T.B. Blues* in 1928 (Columbia 14284-D), while Victoria Spivey had sung her own *T.B. Blues* the year before for Okeh (8494), and she returned to the theme in 1929 (*Dirty T.B. Blues,* Victor V-38570) and 1936 (*T.B.'s Got Me Blues,* Decca 7222). Willie Jackson's song and Jimmie's later composition *Whippin' That Old T.B.* have certain points in common. Both songs mention the infidelity of friends as soon as the disease is diagnosed. Jackson's runs,

T.B.'s alright to have if your friends don't treat you so lowdown,
Don't you ask them for no favours, they even stop hanging around.

While Rodgers sings:

Don't let that old T.B. get you down,
First they want your insurance, then they want to plant you in
the ground.

(Whippin' That Old T.B., Victor 23751)

Rodgers and his new Chrysler sedan in 1931. Right, *with his father and stepmother.*

One wonders if Jimmie had heard Willie Jackson's song before writing his own? His composition is interesting for tuberculosis was, and still is to some extent, a socially unacceptable disease; yet he was quite prepared to admit being a sufferer, and even write songs about it. Victor, of course, in their publicity material about the singer, ignored the fact; and often Jimmie's agents seem to have hushed it up, feeling, perhaps, that it would be harmful to his image. In this respect, it seems surprising that Ralph Peer allowed the recordings to be issued. Perhaps he felt that the public would accept them merely as songs and never realise the link between them and their singer. However, *T.B. Blues* and *Whippin' That Old T.B.* speak much for Jimmie's courage in facing his condition, and for his honesty in recording songs that might well have harmed his public image.

It was a busy time for Jimmie Rodgers, for as well as his benefit work and recordings he was also being invited to many other functions. In March he was invited to appear at the Statewide meeting of the Texas Rotary Club in Austin. He appeared as the featured attraction and was also made an honorary captain in the Texas Rangers. In return, he presented one of his special Weymann guitars to the ranger chief, Adjutant-General William W. Sterling.[16] While in Oklahoma, Jimmie and Carrie were entertained by 'Pawnee Bill' — Major Gordon W. Lillie, the well-known western showman and one-time partner in 'Buffalo' Bill Cody's Wild West Show. Major Lillie had founded a trading post and Indian village at Pawnee, Oklahoma, which, over the years, had become a great tourist attraction. The Rodgerses were invited by Bill to a special luncheon which included buffalo meat. Bill later sent Jimmie a gift of several hunting rifles and a mug which had once been owned by Cody. In May, Jimmie opened

Aspects of Jimmie Rodgers, c. 1931. Above, left, *with Major Gordon W. Lillie ("Pawnee Bill").*

the new Majestic Theatre in San Antonio with a one-week engagement. He was also honoured by being made a special constable in the police force of San Antonio de Bexar — an honour which entitled him to have a police siren on his car. Jimmie, in fact, even used it on official business on one occasion, when he went in pursuit of a traffic violator. He also travelled to Reynosa, Mexico, to open the border radio station XED run by Will Horowitz, the Texan philanthropist and showman. Then in June he was called to a historic recording session in Louisville, Kentucky, where he was to meet and record with the Carter Family — A.P., his wife Sara and sister-in-law Maybelle.

It is surprising that Victor's top country music artists, both discovered at the same Bristol session in 1927, did not meet until almost four years after their initial recordings. However, Ralph Peer had seen the considerable commercial potential of such a coupling, which he eventually arranged for the summer of 1931. The Carter Family, despite their considerable record successes, were never really a part of the show business world in which Jimmie Rodgers moved. The Carters had, of course, wide-ranging experience of radio and concert work, but it was never at the high level at which Jimmie performed. As Porterfield has pointed out,

> Despite the great similarity of their beginnings, however, the Carters and Rodgers thereafter went separate ways — although the divergence was much less evident in their own time than it is now, from the vantage point of time.[17]

Porterfield goes on to point out the differences between their respective followings,

> Although commercially successful, the Carters seem to have had their greatest influence among the more esoteric audiences and artists . . . . [They] also left their indelible stamp on what has come to be known as bluegrass . . . Perhaps of even greater importance is [their] influence upon the new generation of folk 'purists', such as Joan Baez and, to a lesser degree, Bob Dylan.[18]

Rodgers' popularity, by contrast, covered a wide section of the populace and his influence was not only felt in the folk and country music spheres, but had a considerable impact on popular music in general.

Jimmie and the Carter Family were in the Louisville studio on 10 June. The outcome of the day's work was two duets between Jimmie and Sara, both playing guitars: *Why There's a Tear in My Eye* and the only religious song that Jimmie ever recorded, *The Wonderful City*. The following day, Rodgers recorded four takes of a fine blues, *Let Me Be Your Sidetrack*. The first two takes of this song had Clifford Gibson, a black blues guitarist and Louisville resident, providing the lead guitar part. However, Victor chose to issue take 3, which featured Rodgers' solo guitar. A young white steel guitarist was also present at these Louisville sessions: Cliff Carlisle, a

Below, *Cliff Carlisle.* Right, *Rodgers and the Carter Family: Sara, A.P. and Maybelle.*

Kentuckian, who had commenced his recording career with Gennett. Though not widely known at this time, he was soon to become a widely known and well-respected figure in the country music industry, recording prolifically for a number of companies. Carlisle was heavily influenced by the Rodgers style and recorded a number of Jimmie's songs. At the Louisville sessions he accompanied Jimmie on steel guitar in two songs, *When the Cactus is in Bloom* and *Looking For a New Mama*. But the session was to be profitable for him in another respect. During the pre-recording warm-up, Jimmie had been playing round with a verse which ran

> What makes the Shanghai rooster crow for the break of day,
> To let the Dominicker hen know the old rooster's on his way.

Ralph Peer, according to Carlisle,[19] dissuaded Rodgers from making up any more verses for the song as he felt that this type of earthy material might harm Jimmie's image. Rodgers acquiesced and gave what he had to Carlisle, who later completed the song and recorded it for various labels as *Shanghai Rooster Yodel* — which became one of his most popular songs. It seems strange that Peer did not want Jimmie to record this song when only the day before he had recorded *Sidetrack,* a far more earthy and sexually explicit song:

> Let me be your sidetrack until your mainline comes,
> Cause I can do more switching than your mainline ever done.

> When you see a spider climbin' up a wall,
> You can tell the world he's gonna get his ashes hauled.
>
> *(Let Me Be Your Sidetrack,* Victor 23621)

Thus Carlisle's story does not really make sense, at least so far as it concerns the part played by Peer in this curious business; unless of course Jimmie's version of the song was more explicit than the one later recorded by Carlisle.

The same day, Peer arranged for Jimmie and the Carters to record again. This time he visualised two items, mainly dialogue with brief extracts from their more well-known songs. Presumably these were intended more as promotional affairs, to show the various talents of the performers. Sara recalled that Ralph Peer had completely scripted the speech parts to avoid wasting time rehearsing.[20] The first piece was *Jimmie Rodgers Visits the Carter Family.* Three takes were made but presumably fluffed, for they were not issued. Peer then had them try the return match, *The Carter Family Visit Jimmie Rodgers* (or *The Carter Family Interview Jimmie Rodgers).* This resulted in another three takes, none of which were suitable for issue. Following this the session was abandoned for the day.

The next day, Friday, 12 June, *Jimmie Rodgers Visits the Carter Family* was completed in one take. It contains, amongst the dialogue, extracts of three songs, *My Clinch Mountain Home, Hot Time in the Old Town Tonight* and *Little Darling Pal of Mine.* The title of the second Rodgers/Carter side was now changed to *The Carter Family and Jimmie Rodgers in Texas,* and was also completed in one take. The songs featured on this side were a Rodgers solo, *The Yodeling Cowboy,* and a vocal duet with Sara on *T for Texas.* Everyone involved sounds suitably corny and folksy. Jimmie oozes Southern charm and exudes Southern hospitality, offering his guests fried chicken. The Carters act suitably impressed with the Lone Star State and state how nice it is to see their old friend again. Yet these curious items are not without a certain charm. The music, however, is of a much higher standard. Jimmie and Sara on the blue yodel *T for Texas* show that the coupling of Victor's top country artists had tremendous potential; and those hearing these brief duets must surely regret that nothing more along these lines was ever attempted.

Cliff Carlisle was present during these recordings and later spoke about them when being interviewed; but before revealing what lay behind the six unissued takes, asked for the tape-recorder to be switched off. However, it is assumed that A. P. Carter fluffed his lines several times and Jimmie, ill and tired from the continuous recording, voiced a few strong opinions about the mistakes. Even on the takes that were issued, the Carter Family sound fairly uncertain and a little false, A. P. Carter especially so. However, as John Atkins has pointed out, this illustrates the Carters' complete lack of awareness of the show business characteristics that were generally part of a successful recording career.[21]

On 13 and 14 June, Jimmie was presumably resting for nothing was recorded. But on the two following days he was back in the studio to record several more 'experimental' items. *Gambling Polka Dot Blues* and *My Dog Faced Gal* were recorded with Ruth Ann Moore providing a piano accompaniment — which unfortunately adds little to the songs. *Polka Dot Blues* is an extremely good song and was later recorded by Hank Snow early in his career. This features an accompaniment by solo guitar and is, in our opinion, a far more interesting recording than Jimmie's which is seriously hampered by the heavy piano. Inexplicably, *My Dog Faced Gal* was eventually released as *What's It*. The third in this trio of experimentals was *My Good Gal's Gone Blues*. This is more or less a straight blues piece with accompaniment provided by a 'Louisville Jug Band'. This, in fact, was Clifford Hayes' Louisville Jug Band, a group that recorded quite prolifically in its own right. The line-up was Hayes on violin, an unknown clarinettist, Cal and Freddie Smith on guitars and Earl McDonald on jug. (During these Louisville sessions this group also provided accompaniments to the blues singers Ben Ferguson and John Harris.) *My Good Gal's Gone Blues* is a particularly good song and one of Rodgers' better 'experimentals'.

The Rodgerses and the Peers, Kerrville, 1931.

Jimmie with his Model A Ford.

Following his exhausting tour and the long recording session in Louisville, Jimmie returned to Kerrville to recuperate. About this time, he consulted a lung specialist, Dr. I. W. Cooper. Cooper grimly predicted that Jimmie's condition was terminal and so far advanced that another haemorrhage would probably kill him. At most, Dr. Cooper gave Jimmie two more years to live. Probably the doctor's prediction only confirmed what Jimmie knew already. But still he refused to rest more than was absolutely necessary, or to change his lifestyle in any way whatsoever. But certainly he did rest. From October until the end of the year he did little performing and rested as often as Carrie could persuade him to. He never once gave in to his illness or became self-pitying. In fact, Dr. Cooper's diagnosis appeared to have given him added strength to go on fighting the disease. Needless to say, after a brief period of inactivity, Jimmie was soon busy planning another personal appearance tour.

His medical expenses and his passion for high living, as well as his generosity to friends, proved a heavy drain on his finances. Jimmie's earnings were high: probably higher than many purely 'popular' entertainers of the time. Yet his expenses were always higher. So much so, in fact, that Jimmie and Carrie were regretfully planning on selling 'Yodeler's Paradise', their grandiose mansion, in favour of a more modest dwelling. Mrs Rodgers has suggested that the move from Kerrville was because of its location, that it meant a long journey even to attend a recording session in Dallas or San Antonio. Certainly this must have been a contributing factor, for anything that saved Jimmie's energy was to be grasped at; but it seems to us that the main reason for the move was probably financial. The Rodgerses finally decided on a duplex bungalow in San Antonio, at 142 Montclair. With great regret Jimmie and Carrie planned the business of moving house.

While negotiations were taking place for the sale of the house, Jimmie signed a contract with the Leslie E. Kell Tent Theatre Company, another touring tent show operating in the Texas area. From November 1931 until the early part of 1932, Jimmie played engagements with Kell in the Houston/San Antonio area. Also in November, Jimmie received a call from Will Rogers, who asked the singer to meet him at San Antonio's Gunter Hotel for a birthday celebration. Jimmie, of course, was delighted to receive the invitation. Carrie, with all the upheaval of moving house, was unable to go. The following month, the Rodgerses moved from Kerrville, and the Christmas of 1931 was spent in yet another home.

Between 2 and 8 February 1932, eight more titles were added to Jimmie's growing list of recorded material. Rodgers was coupled with a quartet of studio musicians — guitar, mandolin, steel and string bass. The files are again silent regarding personnel but on aural evidence we feel that the steel guitar was played by Charles Kama, with M. T. Salazar on guitar and possibly Jack Barnes on bass. The mandolin may possibly have been played by Rodgers himself. On Bill Halley's composition *Roll Along Kentucky Moon* (recorded on 2 February) and his own composition *Hobo's Meditation* (recorded on the 3rd), Jimmie does not appear to be playing his guitar. Jim Evans, the president of the Jimmie Rodgers Fan Club, felt certain that Jimmie did play mandolin on one of his records but was unfortunately never able to prove it conclusively. Also at this session, Jimmie recorded *My Time Ain't Long* — a strangely prophetic song considering the singer had little more than a year to live. The song deals with the forthcoming execution of a murderer.

> I will go to the gallows at sunrise, they say I am going to hang,
> Through the opening will fall my young body, at the end of a rope
> I will swing.
>
> (*My Time Ain't Long,* Victor 23669)

On this title, co-written by Waldo O'Neal, the mandolin drops out and a barely audible ukulele takes its place. This is almost certainly played by Jimmie. The same instrumentation is used for takes 4 and 5 of *Mississippi Moon,* a song revealing Jimmie's deep affection for his native state,

> I've heard all about the tune that's called the Alabama Moon,
> But the Mississippi moon is just as bright.
>
> (*Mississippi Moon,* Victor 23696)

The final title from 4 February was *99 Year Blues,* written in collaboration with Raymond Hall. Rodgers does not appear to have played guitar on any of the Dallas recordings so far discussed.

On 5 February Jimmie recorded take 6 of *Mississippi Moon* and two takes of *Down The Old Road To Home,* written with Carey Harvey. Both titles have Jimmie playing guitar backed by another, unknown, guitarist. It has sometimes been suggested that this was in fact Oscar Woods, 'The Lone Wolf' — a much underrated blues player. Woods was in Dallas at this time and had recorded four titles with Jimmie Davis on 8 February. However, Woods was a fine musician and the backing on the Rodgers song is, to say the least, mediocre. New research has unearthed a note to the effect that this second guitarist was Fred Coon.

The final titles from the Dallas session were *Blue Yodel No. 10 (Ground Hog Rootin' In My Back Yard),* a song strong in sexual innuendo:

> There's a ground hog rootin' in my back yard at night,
> From the way my mama treats me, he must be rootin' alright.

> I know I ain't no sheik man, don't try to vamp no girls,
> It's my regular grinding that gets me by in this world.
>
> (*Blue Yodel No. 10*, Victor 23696)

and takes 4 and 5 of *Home Call*. The first two takes of this song had been recorded in 1929 with a second guitar and musical saw. The solo guitar version was the one originally issued and is a far superior take of this sentimental ballad. Carrie Rodgers often claimed that this was her favourite song — presumably because of the reference in the text to her and Anita:

> At the close of day, when the sun sinks away,
> Below the western sea,
> Then I'll seek my rest in a little love nest,
> Built for Carrie and 'Nita and me.
>
> (*Home Call*, Victor 23681)

After the session was completed, Jimmie returned to San Antonio. His inactivity was, as always, brief, and he was soon negotiating for a feature program on radio station KMAC.

6 / The Last Blue Yodel

According to Bill Malone, the last year and a half of Jimmie Rodgers' life was filled with recording dates, radio shows, appearances with tent theatres, costly medical treatments and never-realised plans for nationwide tours.[1] It was true that after the Dallas sessions of February 1932 Rodgers was very productive musically, although much of the material recorded was not up to his previously high standard. Ralph Peer was aware of the intensification of the tuberculosis and after the Dallas session sent the following cable to Jimmie:

> Watch your health carefully, as it is worth more than ten-thousand per.[2]

From what we know of Peer as a man and from his relationship with the artistes he managed, the cable can probably be construed as friendly advice. If Rodgers took the time to read it, he certainly did not act upon it and the intensification of the disease coincided with an increase in output and work rate. Soon after the last recording date (6 February 1932), Rodgers left Dallas and rejoined Leslie Kell's Tent Theatre. Jimmie and Kell made elaborate plans for an extensive tour that would take the troupe through the Northwestern states, British Columbia, Canada, New York and back to Texas. These plans never materialised, however, for Rodgers left Kell in March intending to join the J. Doug Morgan Show for a spring and summer tent tour. But Morgan was not to get Rodgers' services either, as Jimmie's failing health forced him to remain in San Antonio for several months.

Slowly, as spring gave way to summer, he regained enough strength to take the job with KMAC in San Antonio. He was employed twice weekly broadcasting from the Bluebonnet Hotel. Jimmie's illness has almost always been given as the reason why he rarely toured outside his native South, and while this may have been true in many cases, there seems good reason to suppose that he often had second thoughts about protracted tours away from the South. In other words, he suffered from homesickness. If he could have had 'his two' with him, he would have undoubtedly made the effort to embark on a long tour. We know that he made a tremendous effort to play one-night stands, fulfil recording dates and make local appearances even when the pain from his disease was obviously excruciating. We feel that homesickness combined with his acute awareness of being 'just an ordinary guy' made him reluctant to play in high-class places. He was far happier on his home ground among the people he knew. Whatever Ralph Peer and Victor had made him, he felt that he was one of them. He sang of the things that troubled or pleased the ordinary man and in a small auditorium or a tent in a Southern town he was at his best. 'If I had money so's I could afford it, I think I'd like nothing better'n just trouping with tent shows all the time', he is supposed to have said to Carrie.[3] Recent research throughout the South has unearthed many 'tonighters' (bills advertising forthcoming one-night stands) announcing 'ADDED ATTRACTION EXTRAORDINARY – WORLD FAMOUS SINGER – JIMMIE RODGERS IN PERSON'. Often the Jimmie is misspelled Jimmy or the Rodgers has become Rogers – occasionally both mistakes were made. Future research into attics and basements will no doubt unearth many more crude, hastily prepared posters which will show that Jimmie was touring extensively even at times when his tuberculosis was raging, and often during the months that he could have been more profitably touring the Northern circuits or even foreign countries.

Rodgers' twice-weekly feature over KMAC proved to be a long engagement. He remained in San Antonio until December 1932, except for the month of August when he was in New Jersey for recordings. A young Texan by the name of Ernest Tubb tuned into the Rodgers radio spots at every available opportunity and, like thousands of others, he began to sing in the same style as his idol. Leon Huff, who later became a featured vocalist with W. Lee O'Daniel's Light Crust Doughboys, was another aspiring singer who is known to have heard the KMAC broadcasts and changed his style to copy Rodgers. Huff soon became known as The Texas Songbird, but it was Tubb who was destined for stardom and longevity in the world of country music. He began his own recording career in 1936 – thanks to the help of Carrie Rodgers (see Chapter 7).

By July 1932 plans had been made by Ralph Peer for Rodgers to travel to Camden, New Jersey, for another recording session. It was at this session that Clayton McMichen played fiddle for Jimmie and the curious relationship between the two men is again raised. McMichen had been a

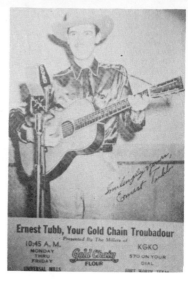

Above, left, *Hank Snow, aged 18.* Right, *Ernest Tubb.* Opposite, *Clayton McMichen* (seated) *and his Georgia Wildcats, 1931: Johnny Barfield, Bert Layne, Hoyt 'Slim' Bryant.*

member of Gid Tanner's Skillet Lickers from 1926, but by 1931 was leading his own band, the Georgia Wildcats. He claimed he met Jimmie in Atlanta in 1926, and certainly the two men obviously knew each other before the 1932 sessions. As discussed earlier, McMichen claimed to have recognised Jimmie's talents when they met in 1926 and subsequently tried to get him a Columbia recording contract. The Columbia people are supposed to have turned down the offer because they already had Riley Puckett. This seems a strange reason as their styles are poles apart. Nevertheless, there could be some element of truth in this and it might explain why Rodgers chose *Sleep, Baby, Sleep* as his first recording when Puckett had already recorded it. On 27 July Rodgers wrote to McMichen to inform him of the plans for the forthcoming session. He begins 'Hello Clayton' and ends 'Your same old pal'.[4] Photographic evidence shows that McMichen and Rodgers had met in 1929 and 1930; it is our opinion that they first met in October 1928 when Rodgers was in Atlanta for a recording session. As an example of how McMichen interpreted his association with Rodgers, we quote from a letter in our possession:

> Now, Jimmie Rodgers. I suppose I knew him better than anyone else (musicians?). He was a sort of happy go lucky guy with little education, I was the only one that ever played fiddle with him on phono recordings. Yes I wrote the words and music to *Peach Picking Time In Georgia* and played it (the fiddle) on the Victor recording with him with Slim Bryant on guitar (one of the finest guitar men in the field). On banjo was Oddie McWilliams [*sic*] a hell of a fine banjo man, and a coloured man on the bass fiddle. I never asked him his name but he was good.[5]

There are mistakes in this hurriedly written letter probably due to the passage of time, but the claim that he was the only man to play fiddle with Rodgers on record is manifestly wrong. Jimmie had recorded in 1929 with a session musician and again in 1931 with Shelly Lee Alley on *Travellin' Blues*. McMichen also seems to be exaggerating when he claims he knew Rodgers well, for it appears that there were few, apart from his family and Ralph Peer, who could lay claim to that.

Jimmie journeyed from Texas via Meridian to Washington D.C. by car. McMichen and the other musicians met him on 5 August and together they travelled to Camden and began rehearsing. The first recordings at this session are a mystery and will always remain so. On 10 August, Rodgers and the four musicians recorded eight takes of *In The Hills Of Tennessee*. Ralph Peer and Eli Oberstein were in attendance at what can only be described as another 'experimental' session. Take 3A was processed as a test but we have been unable to trace a copy and we assume that the end product was destroyed. Why Rodgers' frail body was subjected to such experimentation one will never know. According to the official studio time sheets, this farce took over seven hours. Thus a whole day was wasted in the life of a performer who earlier had publicly admitted 'My time ain't long'. It was also a total waste for the bass player as he appears only to have been used on that day's takes.

On the 11th Rodgers cut four songs with McMichen on fiddle, Oddie McWindows on banjo, and himself on guitar. Jim Evans and Nolan

Porterfield have both questioned whether Jimmie played guitar himself on his later recordings (from approximately the end of 1929). Certainly we can find several instances where their doubts are justified, but in general we feel that Rodgers played guitar on most titles even during his last few sessions. The four songs cut included *Mother, Queen of My Heart,* a song written by Slim Bryant, who was excluded from playing on this day. The song is well performed by Rodgers but suffers from over-sentimentality.

> I had a home out in Texas,
> Down where the bluebonnets grew,
> I had the sweetest old mother,
> How happy we were, just we two.
> Till one day the angels called her,
> That debt we all have to pay,
> She called me close to her bedside,
> These last few words to say ...
>
> (*Mother, Queen Of My Heart,* Victor 23721)

Undoubtedly, Ralph Peer's eyes were on the popular market and it seems safe to say that the majority of the songs Jimmie recorded from August 1932 were chosen by Peer. One has to remember that as well as being Jimmie's friend and recording manager, Peer was the director of a flourishing music publishing company.

The next recording was to become a very expensive mistake on the part of some Victor employee: the company's second inexplicable error in two days. The three men recorded *Prohibition Done Me Wrong,* which Victor never released. The files indicate 'master accidentally destroyed'. The score has never been reproduced in any of Jimmie's song folios, so one is led to assume that the song was written by either Bryant or McMichen. Rodgers was known to like a drink or two and it would seem as if the song poked fun at the unpopular Prohibition laws. If so, it seems likely that Peer may have ordered the matrix destroyed. This may seem farfetched, but Peer was a businessman conscious of the image of his 'star' and mindful of the public to whom he was directing his recordings. Of course, Peer had recorded a number of 'protest' songs by other artists but these were (and were to remain) relatively unknown. It is not beyond the bounds of possibility that Peer allowed the recording to take place and then, with second thoughts at a later date, ordered its destruction. It is not known when the 'accident' took place, but Jimmie's recordings at this time were hot properties (after all, at this stage in his career each one might well have been his last) and every care was taken. No title before or after this was ever damaged in any way. It should also be remembered that Jimmie never recorded the title again nor did he, at any time, record other material which might have been termed political or controversial.

(Fragments of the lyrics of *Prohibition Done Me Wrong* have recently been sighted and it may be said that, in all probability, Rodgers did not bother to rerecord the song not because it was scandalous or controversial but simply because by August 1932 Prohibition was up for repeal and the subject was no longer timely.)

The third title recorded was *Rock All Our Babies to Sleep,* Rodgers' own arrangement of a well-known tune. The song is significant in that it was first recorded by Riley Puckett, on 8 April 1924 (Columbia 107-D). The record made history as the first country recording to feature a yodel. By all accounts, the record sold well, which leads us to wonder if Jimmie learned the song from this recording. Rodgers' own version is not particularly good. The session ended with the sequel to *T.B. Blues* entitled *Whippin' That Old T.B.* (discussed earlier). It was a rousing performance and may have helped others so hospitalised, but at this stage there was little help for the song's composer.

On 15 August Rodgers and his scratch band were back in the studio. By this time McMichen or Rodgers (or both) had convinced Ralph Peer of Slim Bryant's talents as a guitarist, and his distinctive style was added to two of the three titles cut on that day. *No Hard Times* and *Long Tall Mama Blues* were both written by Jimmie and are strong titles in his blues style. They feature contrapuntal runs by banjo and guitar (McWindows and Bryant respectively) while Jimmie plays rhythm guitar, urging the musicians on with the familiar aside, 'pick that thing, boy, pick it'. The titles have a spontaneous ragtime sound, and it is obvious that the players were enjoying themselves. The result was a complete contrast to the rather banal offerings of the earlier session. (*No Hard Times* was apparently logged as a *Blue Yodel* by the ledger clerk and when, years later, officials were consulting the files to prepare a reissue LP they could not trace the item. Many collectors had requested that it be included as the original 78 was scarce and rarely turned up in good condition. The title was duly included on the 'Train Whistle Blues' album, from a privately owned 78 loaned to Victor, who damaged the record; hence the extraneous noises on this track on the album.) The final recording on this day was McMichen's song *Peach Pickin' Time in Georgia,* on which he plays fiddle to Rodgers' guitar and McWindows' banjo. Like many of Jimmie's recordings the song was widely copied, though few stick to the original timing.

The final titles in this series were recorded the following day, with McMichen and McWindows. The haunting strains of Shelly Lee Alley's *Gambling Bar Room Blues* linger in the listener's mind long after the record has ended: a tribute to a fine performance in the unusual key of D minor. Like so many of the aspiring artists whose compositions Jimmie recorded, Alley could not reproduce the magic on his own recordings a few years later. And herein lies the genius of Rodgers, for he had the ability to make almost anything sound special. Peer recognised this, and this was probably why he chose to have Jimmie record with such varied accompaniments, to reach as large an audience as possible. In an effort to diversify, Peer may have dented Jimmie's image as a 'pure' country singer, but it undoubtedly strengthened his claim to greatness as a professional

Jimmie and Carrie, Monmouth Beach, N.J., 1932, while staying with the Peers. Opposite, *Jimmie and Mickey.*

entertainer and helped create a legend.

Rodgers stayed in and around New York after the session and was instrumental in helping McMichen secure a lucrative NBC contract. He was to have worked with them, but after the session Jimmie was exhausted. Interestingly, it was at this session that McMichen claimed he administered Jimmie's morphine injections between takes. Peer, realising that his star charge was failing fast, persuaded him to rest at the Taft Hotel while another session was arranged. This was obviously very hastily arranged by Peer, who was merely intent on building a stockpile of Rodgers recordings: an investment against the day Jimmie's voice would be stilled forever.

The hurriedly arranged session was a strange affair. It consisted of four songs, two of which were written by popular composers, all accompanied by two violins, clarinet, piano and guitar (possibly men from Wayne King's Orchestra who had occupied the studio four days earlier). It is not known why Rodgers was given such strange accompaniment but it may have been to cover up any possible defect in his voice. One cannot trace any fault in the yodelling on these titles, but certainly his voice sounds very tired. The first title, recorded on 29 August, was *In the Hills of Tennessee,* written by Sam M. Lewis and Ira Schuster, both mediocre Tin Pan Alley writers. The song and Rodgers' performance of it could not be called second-rate, although with the bizarre backing it hardly compares with the best of his recorded works. Boston-born popular writer Billy Hill probably holds the record of providing Jimmie with the worst thing he ever recorded. Hill was later to achieve fame with his 1933 composition *The Last Round Up,* but at this time his offering was the dreary and uninspiring *Prairie Lullaby,* which, with the ill-matched backing, makes for a very poor recording. One has to presume, at this late stage in Jimmie's life, that the recording was supposed to be a serious effort by all concerned and thus it cannot be dismissed as a spoof or compared with the tongue-in-cheek *Desert Blues* or *Any Old Time.*

The remaining two titles are somewhat better, although they were also recorded with the same dismal accompaniment. Both were composed by tested writers sympathetic to the Rodgers style. Bill Halley wrote *Miss the Mississippi and You* and Jack Neville co-wrote *Sweet Mama Hurry Home or I'll Be Gone.* Both songs were sentimental love ballads employing a similar type of melody to that used by Gene Austin in the popular music style. As previously mentioned, Austin and Rodgers shared a mutual respect for each other's talents and were good friends. Austin enjoyed great success with his recordings and possibly Rodgers was trying to copy his style or even trying to woo the popular music audience as he had already won over the hillbilly record buyer. His rendition of *Miss the Mississippi and You* is extremely good, and performed with great feeling. *Sweet Mama* is likewise good, but in the mid-'30s Rex Griffin showed what could be done with the song by recording it (for Decca) with solo guitar.

Rodgers, tired and ill, returned to Texas after the session with strict orders to rest. This he did not do, but continued his shows with KMAC. The money that he earned here helped to pay for the private nurse who

now was his constant companion. In October the Rodgers family motored to Meridian for the Williamsons' golden wedding anniversary. Rodgers said:

> Some way I've got a feeling that the next time we're in Meridian — it will be for — a different reason.[6]

The extravert Rodgers obviously felt that the end was near; he never appears to have admitted this before but presumably the celebrations and the fact that they were reunited in the home town proved too much. Carrie Rodgers goes on,

> Was he thinking of his beloved dad? Or had he some premonition that he might —
> Never before had he hinted that any sorrow might be in store for us — for me.[7]

After the anniversary, 29 October, they spent a few days relaxing in Mississippi, and then returned to Texas.

Jimmie returned to KMAC and continued the radio work until the intensification of his disease necessitated his entry into the Baptist Hospital in Houston in January 1933. Fans and friends all over the country sent messages of concern.

> Radio stars like Johnny Marvin broke broadcasting rules to send him through the ether cheery messages; and to dedicate their songs to him — 'To our Jimmie, who's sick down in San Antonio [sic] Texas.'[8]

For his five weeks in hospital Jimmie, as always, made the best of a bad job. His guitar was by his side to charm the nurses with a song, and his Boston Terrier, Mickey, was also a resident, despite the hospital regulations. Upon his discharge he was ordered to rest at home in San Antonio for at least six months. Needless to say, he didn't.

One of the letters he had received in hospital had been from Billy Terrell, an old friend and the tent show operator who had given Jimmie his first opportunity in show business back in 1923. The letter was an urgent appeal for help: Terrell was in trouble. Like many showmen, he had been hard hit by the Depression and between 1929-32 had lost almost $30,000. He contacted Jimmie in the hope that the Blue Yodeler would have some idea of how to help. Jimmie, with typical generosity, cabled Terrell the following reply:

> Am coming as fast as this Cadillac can make it — put in every chair available — charge 75 cents on front seats, 50 cents reserve, 50 cents concert — wire when open.[9]

Terrell opened the show in Paducah, Kentucky, in March 1933, and did as Jimmie had suggested. He cabled Jimmie when everything was ready. Terrell continues the story:

Jimmie and Billy Terrell, Paducah, Kentucky, 1933.

> This was one time I had stage fright. Would they come out that
> Monday night? I owed plenty of bills for paper, candy and
> everything. Imagine my surprise and big thrill of my life when the
> boss canvasman came down to my hotel at five that evening and
> said: 'The front is packed and they are lining up and down the
> sidewalks'. Yes, Jimmie sang and pulled me out of a bad place, and
> then had to go back to Victor for twelve recordings.[10]

Terrell goes on to mention that after Jimmie left the show, business fell
off and he only just managed to finish the season by cutting costs to the
minimum. At the end of the season, he sold out and formed a musical
group which was active on rural theatre circuits until the middle of World
War II.

Even though Jimmie would have been content to play with Terrell's
tent show indefinitely, he realised the need to record again as his finances
were critically low. Private hospital treatment and private medical staff
had sadly depleted his funds. By April 1933, even the ever-optimistic
Rodgers knew that he could not last much longer. His main concern was to
provide for 'his two' and he wanted his wife and daughter to have
something laid by when the inevitable happened. He had received a
lucrative offer from Brunswick and as his contract with Victor was about
to expire he arranged a meeting with Ralph Peer. He mentioned this to
Carrie:

> Goin' to New York, Mother. Old contract's up. Gotta talk it over
> with Ralph. See what he thinks about that Brunswick offer. Won't
> take it, though, if Victor meets it. Victor — they've been fine to me.
> Only thing is — gotta have more money. Doctors, nurses, hospitals —
> doggone! They cost a lot, don't they? [11]

The Victor contract was renewed and Ralph Peer organised a long lease
on the New York studios. Rodgers' previous session had been in August
1932 and Peer was obviously waiting for the day that Jimmie would be
strong enough to record again. Jimmie never was really strong enough but
decided to make the trip anyway. Probably both he and Peer realised that
this would be the last session. From the Sunset Station in San Antonio,
Jimmie and his nurse boarded a Southern Pacific express to meet the SS
Mohawk at Galveston, where the ocean voyage to New York would
commence. Carrie could not make the journey with them because her
brother Covert, who was also ill, was coming to stay in Texas. That was
one reason, but probably the finances would not stretch to a third fare to
New York. Carrie's only reminder of Jimmie was Mickey, the Boston
Terrier who also had his own scrapbook of fan mail since Jimmie had let
him 'talk' into the microphone at the radio stations.

When Rodgers arrived in New York he was introduced to two young
songwriters, Dwight Butcher and Lou Herscher, who were on Ralph Peer's
books at Southern Music. Both were from East Tennessee and had
journeyed to the city in search of recording contracts. Butcher had cut a
few titles for Crown Records and Peer had signed him as a Victor artist.
Rodgers had often said that he wanted to die with his boots on and not
counting the flies crawling up a hospital wall; now he told Butcher that if
he lived long enough he would record some of his songs. He expressed
interest in several titles and spent some time working through the scores.
One in particular, called *Old Love Letters (Bring Memories of You),*
interested him. From Lou Herscher's folio of compositions he chose *I'm
Free from the Chain Gang Now.*

Old Love Letters was not a new song, as Dwight Butcher explained to
us,

> Now about *Old Love Letters.* When this song was first placed with
> Southern Music, they had Kate Smith in mind to do the song. She
> heard it and was interested in doing the song, but for some reason
> did not perform it right away. This was early 1933 I believe. I did
> not record it for the reason that Mr Peer wanted to make a pop song
> out of it, and at this time, as you probably know, JR was doing that
> type of number. After Jimmie recorded it, I just didn't feel like
> doing the number anymore. So that's about the story on that
> song. [12]

This information came from Dwight Butcher in response to a query as
to why he did not record the song at the time. It contains many interesting
facts, but particularly the reference to Jimmie Rodgers and 'pop' music.

Dwight Butcher in 1931.

Butcher was raised in East Tennessee and was familiar with homegrown mountain music; if his opinion of Rodgers was that he was a 'popular' singer, then it could well be that Rodgers considered himself a popular entertainer and not a hillbilly artist.

Jimmie invited Dwight to his room at the Taft Hotel and selected several other Butcher compositions: *Down in the Lone Star State, Oh, Mama, Why Didn't I Listen to You, When the Sun Hides Away for the Day* and *Sunset Time in Sunny Tennessee.* But these were never recorded. Butcher recalled that Jimmie was propped up on a bed with several pillows behind him and that his nurse was in constant attendance. One wonders how much energy Rodgers spent in rehearsing these songs. Although he enjoyed singing these sentimental and hauntingly melodic songs, Ralph Peer and Jimmie's public were anxiously awaiting more Blue Yodels. Thus, on 17 May, the studio was made ready for a recording of *Barefoot Blues,* later numbered 12 in the enduring blue yodel series. A cot was set up in the studio and between takes, Jimmie would rest until he had regained enough strength to continue.

Bill Malone has suggested that this last session 'is one of the most heart-rending episodes in Show-Business history'.[13] And while this may well be true, there is a certain cold-bloodedness about the business. Rodgers probably realised that this would be his last session but he was determined to leave his family well provided for. It would seem that he viewed the situation quite calmly and the end product seems like an unusual insurance policy. The recording engineers had to be on their best form, for any mistake on their part would mean the scrapping of a whole take. Most of the Rodgers material at this session was cut in only one take, and only a few titles were afforded the luxury of a second cut. It must have been a great strain on everyone concerned, but the greatest strain was on Jimmie himself. But in his usual role of master showman, few would detect physical exhaustion in his voice on the songs from this session. The first day produced four titles, all with Jimmie's guitar as their sole accompaniment. It is interesting to note that Rodgers almost certainly played his own guitar at this session. Earlier we have intimated that despite his personalised style and his occasional sizzling runs, Jimmie had never been happy with his guitar work. The discerning listener may notice that Jimmie played less on his post-1929 records, though he always did on the blue yodels and on similar blues-based pieces. Now, however, at his last session, he was relying on his own ability. In addition to *Barefoot Blues* he also recorded *Dreaming with Tears in My Eyes,* a ballad co-written with Waldo O'Neal; *The Cowhand's Last Ride,* a much underrated original composition; and *I'm Free from the Chain Gang Now,* written by Lou Herscher and Saul Klein. The quality of his singing and yodelling were as good as ever and few people would know that as he sang he must surely have wondered how many more performances could be forced from his ravaged lungs.

On the second day, 18 May, Jimmie was again in the studio; he recorded a second take of *Dreaming with Tears in My Eyes* and two new songs, all with his own guitar accompaniment. The first take of *Dreaming with Tears in My Eyes* was issued on the original 78 release (Bluebird B-7600), but when the time came for the LP reissues in the 1950s the second take was used. We personally feel that the first version was superior as the timing is quite different on the second take. However, both are perfectly good recordings in their own right and why Jimmie had to waste energy in remaking the song remains yet another mystery. It is particularly

The Jimmie Rodgers Picture Record (Victor 18-6000), issued in 1933. The reverse side is Blue Yodel No. 12.

strange in view of the fact that the first take provided the original release, which surely suggests that it was totally satisfactory. The two new songs cut that day were both Rodgers' compositions. One of these, *Yodelling My Way Back Home,* contains a mistake which was ignored by the session director. Jimmie, probably in great pain, suffered a momentary lapse of concentration at the start of the yodel and the hesitation is marked, but the record was issued. The last song recorded on this day was *Jimmie Rodgers' Last Blue Yodel* — a fine song and a fitting end to the great blue yodel series.

Two days later, Jimmie returned to the studio. Peer had obviously advised him against recording and had set up a session for the following week. He had also hired backing musicians. Rodgers, however, obviously insisted on utilising all his available time and persuaded Peer to set the wheels in motion for another solo session. Two takes were recorded of *The Yodelling Ranger* and *Old Pal of My Heart.* In March 1931 Jimmie had been made an honorary Texas Ranger and was extremely proud of this. With Ray Hall, who had already co-written a few songs with him, Jimmie wrote *The Yodelling Ranger.* The song was widely issued in the US, England and Australia, but when the LP reissues were put together this song was overlooked. Perhaps it was confused with his *Yodelling Cowboy,* but whatever the reason it remained unissued and a highly sought-after item until recently. *Old Pal of My Heart* is one of those 'pure corn' songs with a Gene Austin-style melody line which sounds mundane when recorded by anyone else. The song was co-written by John B. Mason, yet another unknown but talented composer with whom Jimmie was briefly connected. Rodgers has been credited with the co-authorship of a vast proportion of his later recorded songs, but just how much he contributed remains a matter for speculation. After the session, exhausted, he was taken back to the Taft Hotel with strict orders to rest for three days. This time he obeyed the order — he was too weak to argue.

On 24 May, however, he was back in the studio and four titles were cut. With John Cali on steel guitar and Tony Colicchio on guitar, Rodgers recorded the Butcher/Herscher song *Old Love Letters.* This has a beautiful melody, but one can detect that Jimmie had trouble in finding enough breath for the yodel. Unknown to Butcher at this time, this was the only song Jimmie recorded from the batch he had selected from his folio. Calle changed to banjo for the sprightly *Mississippi Delta Blues,* co-written with Jack Neville. The song contains some extremely difficult chord changes but its appeal lies in the fact that it endorses Jimmie's deep love for his Southern homeland: the homeland he knew he would never see again.

> There's a feeling I can't lose, that muddy water's in my shoes,
> When I get that Mississippi Delta blues.
> *(Mississippi Delta Blues,* Victor 23816)

Both Cali and Colicchio played guitars to accompany Jimmie's singing and yodelling on *Somewhere Down Below the Dixon Line,* written with Jack Ryan and again a vivid portrayal of 'how great life was down South'. Rodgers was now having to rest for longer periods between takes, and his strength was failing fast. However, he dispensed with the other musicians and with solo guitar recorded *Fifteen Years Ago Today.* This proved to be the last song that Jimmie ever recorded. (When it was released, some versions used the alternative title *Years Ago.*)

On 25 May Rodgers rested in his hotel room and next day he went on a sight-seeing tour of Coney Island with his nurse. Whilst there he suffered an attack of spasms. He was rushed back to his hotel but died during the early hours of 26 May 1933. Carrie Rodgers was informed by telephone the following morning. In her own words:

Six-o-clock in the morning!
The telephone – ringing – ringing – ringing –!
Long distance – New York calling.
Calling Mrs. Jimmie Rodgers!
Hotel Taft
Tubercular pneumonia – [14]

The Victor officials were stunned into complete silence, even though they must have realised that his death was both inevitable and imminent. As a mark of respect, the studios were closed for the morning of the 27th. This was how Dwight Butcher learned of Jimmie's death. He had not heard from the singer or from Peer for several days, and, anxious to know how many of his songs Jimmie had recorded, went to the studio. The desk clerk told him of Rodgers' death. Within two days, he and Lou Herscher had written *When Jimmie Rodgers Said Goodbye*. In the following chapter we shall discuss this and other tribute records to Jimmie, for never before did the death of a recording artist cause such a wave of recorded tributes.

We might observe at this point that no one has ever discovered a Rodgers composition that he did not record. In his last two years he used fewer of his own compositions and began to rely more and more on the work of Tin Pan Alley writers. Usually, Jimmie was credited as co-author, but it is to be assumed that he did little more than change a note or two here or a phrase or word there; as indeed was the case with the Butcher song *Old Love Letters*. The profitable and highly successful partnership with Elsie McWilliams had virtually dissolved by the end of 1929 – the year, we would suggest, that Ralph Peer began to exert more and more influence on Jimmie's musical direction.

On 27 May the *New York Times* carried two paragraphs announcing Jimmie's death. This appeared on page 13, and we reproduce it here with all its mistakes.

RADIO SINGER DIES

James C. Rogers of 'Hill Billy' fame succumbs in hotel here.
James C. Rogers of San Antonio, Texas, a singer of 'Hill-Billy' songs on the radio, died at noon yesterday at the Hotel Taft. He was 35 years old. According to friends, he had been suffering from tuberculosis for the last ten years and had come to New York two weeks ago, accompanied by a nurse, to fill a phonograph recording engagement.

Mr Rogers is survived by his widow, Mrs Carrie Rogers, and a daughter, Anita, who are in San Antonio. His body will be shipped there tonight for burial. He was a native of Meridian, Miss., the son of Aaron W. Rogers.

Even his own hometown paper, the Meridian *Star,* suffered from mistakes in his obituary. This appeared in the 26 May edition, on the front page, beginning:

JIMMY RODGERS
SINGER-YODLER
DIES SUDDENLY

Information reaching Meridian of the death of Jimmie Rodgers, which occurred in New York Friday at 6 a.m. came as a shock to friends and relatives here.

Mr. Rodgers, aged 36, famous 'blues' singer and yodler, was in New York making records for the Victor Company . . .

Nate Williamson, Jimmie's brother-in-law and a lawyer, arranged the funeral transport. As the train completed the long journey from New York to Meridian, multitudes of people gathered at Union Station to pay their respects to the young man who lay in the baggage car. It was late at night when the train arrived, but as it pulled into Meridian the engineer, Homer Jenkins, blew the whistle in in a long wail until the train halted. This was

The Singing Brakeman.

the train crew's own tribute to the Singing Brakeman who loved to hear
the lonesome sound of an engine's whistle.

Then — like a part of the night itself, a low, mellow train whistle.
Not the usual 'whoo-whoo-oo', but a whistle that was not a whistle.
A long, continuous moaning that grew in volume as the train crept
towards me along the silver rails.

'Whoo-oo-oo-oo-oo-'

Continuous; never ceasing until the powerful engine breathed to a
rest and the drivers ceased turning.

Tribute! The train crew; engineer, fireman, all of them
remembered how Jimmie Rodgers had loved train whistles.[15]

After the funeral services, Jimmie Rodgers was laid to rest beside
his daughter, June Rebecca, in the Oak Grove Cemetary.

7/ Jimmie Rodgers in Retrospect

It was a cold dreary day in New York City,
In the year nineteen hundred and thirty three.
'He's arriving by boat from Galveston,' they said,
'He's not in good health, you see.'
I had heard talk, here and there, for several years now
That he was suffering from the dreaded old TB,
But the courage and will he had to live and sing,
You wondered how this could be.

I was just a young boy from the mountains,
Way over in east Tennessee,
I came up to New York for the Victor Company
In that year nineteen hundred and thirty three.
I guess I was a lucky young fella
To be making recordings that year.
We were both under contract to a great music man
A fellow named R. S. Peer.

I'll never forget the rainy morning
He came over from the Taft Hotel;
A nurse walking closely beside him,
It would sure be the end if he fell.
A smile and a handshake from this great man,
I could see no sympathy needed here.
We talked for an hour or so of his trip
And occasionally the nurse would appear.

We finally got down to the music business,
And I sang him a few of my songs.
He picked up his famous old Martin guitar,
As I sang, he just strummed along.
He smiled now and then as he listened.
'Kid', he said, 'Can I change a word or two?'
Then his thin trembling hand held the manuscript
Of *Old Love Letters Bring Memories of You.*

In his room at the Taft Hotel that night
I helped him rewrite my song.
He said, 'I'll record it tomorrow, Kid:
That is, if I live that long.'

The song you're listening to, my friend,
Has a story behind each note.
The last song Jimmie Rodgers recorded,
I'm proud to say I wrote.

(Dwight Butcher, *Jimmie Rodgers in Retrospect* [Cert Records, 1969])

Jimmie Rodgers was dead; and probably few realised the enormous influence that the Singing Brakeman would wield over the subsequent development of country music, or that his popularity would not diminish in any way with his death. Victor had a considerable stock of unissued material which would be presented to the public at intervals, and this would serve to keep his name before the public for at least several years to come. Yet the memory of Jimmie Rodgers was to be perpetuated in a more important way. His influence on the musical style of successive generations of singers was to become increasingly obvious. And of considerable interest here is the fact that many of these singers recorded their own tributes to Jimmie. Almost certainly this was the first time that tribute songs had been recorded at the death of a hillbilly musician; and they were among the first recorded tributes for any singer in the whole field of popular music. Today, the practice is a common one: a singer dies, tributes from his fellow performers are recorded, but within a short time the records are deleted and forgotten. The significant point regarding the tributes to Rodgers is that they began to appear in the month following his death and continued to appear at intervals until the 1960s and even later. These recordings range from sincere attempts to acknowledge a debt to Jimmie and his music to the morbid and over-sentimental, cashing in on a still commercially successful property.

One of the first of these tributes on the market was Gene Autry's *The Life of Jimmie Rodgers* backed with *The Death of Jimmie Rodgers.* These songs were both from the pen of that prolific country music songwriter Bob Miller, and were recorded on 22 June 1933. In emotive voice, and backed by a mournful violin, Autry sang:

> The angels have taken you, Jimmie, to God in his wisdom and love,
> For they needed another sweet singer to blossom in heaven above.
> There are millions who'll miss you, friend Jimmie;
> Miss the sad voice that made millions happy,
> May God in his mercy grant your friends their one prayer,
> That they'll meet you friend Jimmie up there.
>
> (Gene Autry, *The Death of Jimmie Rodgers*, Perfect 12922)

The advertisement sheet for the record advertised the songs as by 'Gene Autry — Jimmie's friend', though the two men had never met.

Bob Miller, with Carson Robison and Andrew Jenkins, was one of the most prolific writers of 'event' songs in the hillbilly repertoire. Miller began his career by writing epitaphs for an undertaker in Memphis in 1906, when he was only 11 years old. This early training probably inspired him to have 'epitaphs in song' ready for almost any event. Miller also laid claim to the gift of second-sight, and prophesied Huey Long's death two years before he was shot. However, in his tribute songs for Jimmie Rodgers Miller was probably inspired by the Butcher-Herscher composition *When Jimmie Rodgers Said Goodbye*. Sheet music copies of this were soon published by the F.B. Haviland Music Co., and many were mailed to radio stations and newspapers who were unaware of Rodgers' death until they received the song.[1] Butcher and Herscher recorded the song for Crown some time in June. It would obviously have been released as soon as possible; and almost certainly before the Autry coupling mentioned above.

Gene Autry was given the score of *When Jimmie Rodgers Said Goodbye* by the publishers and recorded it himself on 1 November 1933, with guitar and violin accompaniment. For the reverse of the record, Autry chose his own composition of *Good Luck Old Pal* (which was copyrighted as *Goodbye Old Pal* in 1934). This song follows the pattern of Jimmie's own blue yodels, and is probably the most interesting of all the tribute songs. A

Three recorded tributes that followed Rodgers' death and Garner Eckler and Roland Gaines' version of Moonlight and Skies, *made in 1934. They were later popular on the Renfro Valley Barn Dance.*

superior version to Autry's was recorded for Gennett by Kenneth Houchins in the spring of 1934. With only guitar accompaniment, Houchins sang and yodelled in a style very reminiscent of Rodgers:

> I just received a message, Jimmie that you were gone,
> And my heart aches with sorrow as I sing this lonesome song.
> (Kenneth Houchins, *Goodbye Old Pal,* Champion 16793)

The next few years saw many such tributes, including *Memories of Jimmie Rodgers* by W. Lee O'Daniel and his Lightcrust Doughboys. This recording has a strong lyric and fine singing by Leon Huff. Bradley Kincaid and Asher Sizemore & Little Jimmie followed with tributes. In October 1936, Mrs Carrie Rodgers recorded *We Will Miss Him When Evening*

Shadows Fall for Bluebird, with the young Ernest Tubb backing her on Jimmie's own Martin guitar. A day later Tubb recorded his own tribute. Later, in the postwar years, came recordings by Jimmie Skinner, Jimmie Walker and Hank Snow with his son Jimmie Rodgers Snow. Ernest Tubb and Snow were largely instrumental in arranging the first Jimmie Rodgers Memorial Day celebrations in Meridian, in 1953, and to mark the occasion Tubb recorded yet another tribute song. One side of the record is interesting, for *Jimmie Rodgers' Last Thoughts (My Bluebonnet Dream)* was co-written by Elsie McWilliams.

1953 also saw the tragic death of that other influential giant of hillbilly music, Hank Williams. Thus, it was obvious that the two singers would be linked in tasteless tributes designed to appeal to the widest possible audiences. These songs followed the 'Will Hank Williams Meet Jimmie Rodgers in Heaven?' pattern.[2] One of the latest and perhaps most interesting tributes appeared in 1969. This was Dwight Butcher's poem *Jimmie Rodgers in Retrospect,* which heads this chapter. The poem, narrated over Jimmie's recording of *Old Love Letters,* recounts the meeting between Butcher and Rodgers shortly before the latter's death. These many tributes and, more importantly, the many singers who modelled themselves on Rodgers' style to a greater or lesser extent, testify to his wide popularity. Just how wide-ranging this was is well worth examining, for it has been suggested that at his death Jimmie was almost unknown outside his native South.

In a somewhat ambiguous statement in his Meridian *Star* article, Ralph Peer wrote,

> Jimmie was practically unknown north of the Mason-Dixon Line, but within a year he became the most important recording artist in the region where Hillbilly Music has always enjoyed greatest popularity.[3]

That region is presumably the South; but in the light of other evidence the statement is unbelievable. One could not deny that Rodgers was immensely popular in the rural South, but was he really almost unknown in the North?

In Canada, in the early '30s, Jimmie's records influenced many singers and acted as the spur for at least half a dozen young men to follow a career in music singing in the Rodgers style. Rodgers was also influential on Australian singers. In Britain, from 1928 onwards, Zonophone and Regal Zonophone pressed his records in large numbers for sale to British fans. The British companies even pressed an international series for sale in Africa – another continent where Jimmie had many admirers. In view of this evidence of international recognition it seems absurd to believe that he had only local or regional appeal in his own country.

Nolan Porterfield has met the present owner of 'Yodeler's Paradise' and discovered that his father was an avid Rodgers collector in the '30s. He

SUPREME EDITION

Jimmie Rodger

AMERICA'S BLUE YODELER

ALBUM OF
SONGS

INCLUDING

"MOTHER, THE QUEEN OF MY HEART"

"PEACH PICKING TIME DOWN IN GEORGIA"

"A DRUNKARD'S CHILD"

"THE MYSTERY OF NUMBER 5"

"WAITING FOR A TRAIN"

AS WRITTEN AND SUNG ON VICTOR RECORDS BY

JIMMIE RODGERS

SOUTHERN MUSIC PUB. CO.,
1619 BROADWAY   NEW YORK

lived then near Chicago.[4] Gene Autry, between the years 1929-33, worked almost exclusively in the North (New York or Chicago) and it seems strange that he would so closely follow Rodgers' style and material if the latter was almost unknown there. These may be isolated examples, of course, but it seems unlikely that Ralph Peer would have arranged a tour of Northern circuits if Jimmie had been unknown: Peer was too shrewd a businessman to risk such a venture. Carrie Rodgers seems to corroborate our assumption when she wrote of this proposed Northern tour:

> He was unable to make the tours which had been arranged for him through the northern states and Canada. Had he been physically able to make those personal appearance tours, the Northland, as well as the Southland, would have lost their hearts to the yodeling singer 'in person', as they had already to that silvertone voice on the phonograph records and radio.[5]

This would seem to indicate that Jimmie's records sold well, if not very well, in the North. It seems, really, as if his records sold well wherever there were record dealers. But as we have suggested, his widest popularity was to be found in the rural South and Southwest. After all, the old legend has it that even at the height of the Depression, customers in rural general stores would place an order for 'a pound of butter, a dozen eggs, and the latest Jimmie Rodgers record'.[6]

It should be borne in mind that most of Jimmie's recording career, and certainly the years that saw his greatest successes, were the years of the worst economic depression that America had ever known: a period, moreover, that saw a dramatic decline in record sales. For example, in 1927 sales figures show that 104 million records were sold. By 1932 sales had dropped to the meagre total of six million. Yet while many hillbilly artists were allowed to fade into obscurity, Jimmie's discs were selling in their thousands. How many thousands, though, has never been revealed. Exaggerated claims have suggested that every Rodgers record sold a million, but this is clearly nonsense. Bill Malone has estimated that a possible 20 million of his records had been sold by 1933.[7] However, the exact sales figures may never be known, for a fire at the Camden warehouse, where the Victor sales data was stored, has destroyed most chances of checking. The fire also destroyed any means of discovering how many of Jimmie's records were sold in the Northern states. A comparison of Northern and Southern sales figures would have proved of great interest in any discussion of Jimmie's popularity.

Bearing in mind the Depression background against which his recording career took place; the severe illness which frequently incapacitated him and made public appearances dependent upon the state of his health; the fact that the appearances he did make were almost exclusively in the South or Southwest, and that he had little personal management and no vast publicity machine like today's performers', we can only describe his popularity as phenomenal. We feel that there are at least four reasons which may help to explain this amazing popularity. First, a wide-ranging repertoire which in some ways reflected the era in which he lived. Secondly, a desire among record buyers of the time for new styles and material. Thirdly, his symbolising the restlessness of spirit admired by most Americans. Lastly, sympathy for his severe illness. We shall discuss each possibility in turn.

Jimmie's repertoire was extremely wide-ranging in both style and content: far wider than any rural performer's before him. Sentimental ballads such as *Daddy and Home* and *Mother Queen of My Heart*; narrative songs; the novelty material like *My Dog Faced Gal* and *Everybody Does It in Hawaii*; and of course the blues-based and risqué material. All these were accompanied in a wide variety of musical styles and instrumental combinations — solo guitar, Hawaiian, jazz, and novelties like musical saws and railroad whistles. Thus, in this tremendous variety, there was something for almost every musical taste. In this respect, Ralph Peer's 'experimental' sessions could not have been more successful. This material, presented in Jimmie's inimitable and polished style, with the sincerity evident in all his recordings, must have pleased many popular record buyers and not merely those who followed the hillbilly market. Then we must also consider that Rodgers was a master at presenting the blues in a form palatable to white audiences. His material had less of the raw aggression and primitive drive of black song, yet still it managed to convey the 'lowdown' feeling which white audiences expected (and in most cases still expect) of the blues. The recordings echoed the era through which he lived: an era of hard times, breadlines and hand-outs. Without specifically referring to the problems of his time, Jimmie Rodgers conveyed the feeling of the late '20s and early '30s.

A second reason which we would like to suggest is that the public were prepared for something new when Jimmie Rodgers hit the market. It would seem that the string band, with its traditional repertoire, had dominated the hillbilly record market for the five years since its birth. One can reply, of course, that there were commercially successful records by solo artists — Riley Puckett, Vernon Dalhart, Ernest Thompson and so forth — but this does not detract from the argument that the greatest sales during that period were enjoyed by the string bands: Charlie Poole's North Carolina Ramblers, Gid Tanner's Skillet Lickers, and a number of bands led by Ernest Stoneman. Five years is a considerable time for any particular style of performing to hold sway with its audience, and there is no reason to think that hillbilly music was any exception. It should also be borne in mind that the two decades following World War I were times of great change and innovation in the entertainment world: an era of 'fads' and 'crazes', rapidly sweeping the country and just as rapidly forgotten. Thus, when Jimmie Rodgers offered the hillbilly record-buyer something new, a variation on a traditional theme, it was eagerly accepted. For the popular record buyer, Rodgers offered an unusual, perhaps novel, sound sensation. For it must be remembered that in order to sell the amount of records that he did, and to have had the following that he had, Jimmie's popularity must have extended far beyond the narrow confines of the rural record-buying market.

The third possibility that should be discussed has its roots in Kenneth Allsop's admirable study of the American migrant worker, *Hard Travellin'*. Allsop suggests that Americans have a unique kind of mobility; that America is a nation where 'restlessness is pandemic; entrenchment means fossilization, a poor spirit'. This is a large generalisation and many exceptions could be made, but many Americans do seem to have this tremendous restlessness, the desire to 'top the next hill' in a spirit of 'endless quest'.[8] If this argument is acceptable, then it may go a long way in explaining Rodgers' amazing popularity. Jimmie Rodgers, with his railroad background and the romantic railroad imagery of many of his songs, personified this 'wandering spirit' — the rounder who found fame and fortune — another element in the American Dream. It is significant that Victor used this 'wanderer' image in their publicity material:

> He wandered about the Country, his guitar and voice providing the necessities of life.[9]

With this imagery and his own talent, how could Jimmie not be successful?

The final possibility that should be mentioned, although one with little to recommend it, we feel, is sympathy for his chronic illness, and admiration for his courage in the running battle with 'that old TB'. However, this explanation requires that the vast majority of his audience should have been aware of his fight against the disease. Neither Victor nor his personal publicity mentioned his illness, mainly because of the social stigma of tuberculosis. And although Rodgers himself made no secret of the fact that he was a victim, we feel that few of the general public would have known of his affliction. Friends, fellow-musicians, and the few who linked his TB songs and cancelled appearances would have known, but this minuscule percentage could in no way have affected his record sales.

It is worthwhile mentioning here the more obvious reasons why Jimmie was more popular in the South. Jimmie was first and foremost a Southerner and the South is nothing if not loyal to its own. Jimmie returned this loyalty in many ways, extolling the virtues of the South in many of his songs and paying tribute to Southern states — *Mississippi Moon, Miss the Mississippi and You, Mississippi Delta Blues, My Carolina Sunshine Girl, In the Hills of Tennessee, Peach Picking Time in Georgia, Roll Along Kentucky Moon, T for Texas*, and *Dear Old Sunny South By the Sea*. And, of course, his tours of the major circuits were confined to the South or Southwest. Finally, we should remember that the traditional home of hillbilly music is in that area.

These possible explanations may help us to understand Jimmie Rodgers' popularity with English-speaking audiences; but what was the

FOR THE SAKE OF DAY'S
        GONE BYE — Waltz

過ぎし日のために
(J. Rodger:-Jack White)

ROLL ALONG KENTUCKY
          MOON — Waltz

ケンタッキーの月
(Bill Halley)

'Jimmie Rodgers, Vocal
with Guitars

アメリカのバラード・シンガー、ジミー・ロジャースの生涯は、ウェスター
ンミュジックの大空を輝かしくよぎつた慧星にたとへられませう。ロジャース
が大衆の間で歌つた六年（1927—1933）に、彼ははかり知れない喜びと慰め
を愛し理解する人々に與へました。ロジャースを聞く人々にとつては、彼
のブルースとヨーデルは日々の生活の苦しさ厄介ごとを笑つてこたえるための
力となつてゐたのです。ロジャースは、人々の中で育ち、その人々の膿よりも
熱心に働き、人々の歌をロジさむ間に愛えたので、一番良く大衆の心を知つて
ゐたのです。

ロジャースはミシシッピー・メリデアンの鐵道工夫長の家に生れ、彼自身
も、十四の時から鐵道で働き始め、以後十四年間、健康を損ふ日まで働き続け

A-1430

quality of his music which so appealed to people of diverse languages and cultures? In India, many Rodgers records were released on the HMV and Twin labels. While many of these would have been bought by the resident European population, it would be wrong to assume that the Indian market for his records was entirely composed of Europeans. A correspondent of John Greenway's reported seeing a collection of Jimmie's records in an Eskimo's hut at Point Barrow.[17] Jimmie has had a loyal band of followers in Japan for many years, and his popularity in Africa seems amazingly widespread. Many collectors have testified to seeing his records in African villages, especially in South and East Africa. Blues authority Paul Oliver has related a fascinating story regarding the Kipsigi tribe of East Africa. Among this people, Jimmie Rodgers occupies the position of a demi-god, whose invocation, addressed to the spirit of 'Chemirocha', may be heard on the record 'Music of Africa — Kenya' (Decca LF1121). Oliver continues the story:

> In his introduction to the song, the collector, Hugh Tracey, explains that it is only within the last few years that the Kipsigis have heard the gramophone. The performer who specially took their fancy was Rodgers, who seemed to them a formidable player on their local *chepkong* lyre, and Kipsigi girls have come to believe that Jimmie Rodgers is a kind of centaur, half man, half antelope. In their song *Chemirocha,* they seductively invite him to dance with them.[11]

What the quality is in Jimmie's music that so appeals to non-European audiences can only be guessed at, but further research into this aspect of his popularity would certainly yield some fascinating material.

We have, thus far, suggested some reasons or possible explanations for Rodgers' popularity. But we must now examine Jimmie's effect on the development of country music. What exactly was his influence on the fledgeling hillbilly recording industry? It has sometimes been suggested that he was solely responsible for making an unsophisticated, limited-appeal music into the billion-dollar industry that it now is. To assign all this responsibility to Jimmie Rodgers is to overstate the case. Yet he was probably more influential than any other single artist. Jimmie Rodgers was the first country-based performer to achieve some degree of national and international recognition, and the first to receive much attention from the popular music industry's trade press. Undoubtedly, many must have considered Rodgers to be more a popular singer than a hillbilly singer, and perhaps some may hold this view today. It could, perhaps, be argued that

Rodgers' recordings outside the United States. Top right, *a Japanese Victor release, with its accompanying leaflet* (top left). Centre, *releases to the Indian (Twin) and West African (Zonophone) markets.* Bottom, *the British Regal Zonophone issue of the two-part* Jimmie Rodgers Medley, *a 1935 reprocessing of six of Rodgers' hits, issued in Britain, Eire, Australia and India but never in the USA.*

only the manner of his discovery and his early records won him a place within the hillbilly category. Rodgers recorded little material of a traditional nature and certainly many of his accompaniments would fall into the popular style. But whether Rodgers was a country singer or not is a difficult question, for it necessitates an acceptable definition of what hillbilly music is; and there is, as yet, no satisfactory definition. As Porterfield has put it:

> Never from its beginnings adequately defined or limited, 'hillbilly' now seems lost and dissolved in a maze of musical types known variously as 'folk', 'cowboy', 'country-western' . . . 'western swing' and 'bluegrass'. [12]

Any attempted definition of hillbilly would involve factors such as period of recording, nature of material, instrumentation, geographical location and so on. Yet so many variations could be noted in these factors as to make any attempted definition worthless. To determine whether Jimmie Rodgers might legitimately be styled a hillbilly performer one could compare his style and choice of material with performers who are generally accepted members of that field. However, because of Jimmie's unique material and original style, this also raises considerable problems. Rather unsatisfactorily, one might suggest a comparison with Riley Puckett. Puckett, the featured singer of Gid Tanner's Skillet-Lickers and a highly successful solo performer, recorded a considerable amount of traditional material but also delved into the realm of the vaudeville and popular repertoire. Puckett's songs were mainly accompanied by solo guitar or guitar and mandolin, but he was also the vocalist for Clayton McMichen's pop-orientated band the Melody Men. Puckett, like Rodgers, toured with tent shows, but unlike Rodgers was a frequent performer at the traditional fiddle contests. He rarely appeared at legitimate variety theatres. However, had the opportunity presented itself, Puckett would undoubtedly have entertained at those venues as much as Rodgers. It was chance more than intention that made Jimmie a featured attraction in 'real' theatres. This brief and rather poor comparison shows, we hope, that although Jimmie Rodgers achieved a far wider popularity than Puckett, or for that matter any other accepted hillbilly singer, there are sufficient similarities to substantiate the argument that he was a hillbilly artist: but a country performer whose appeal reached far beyond the rather narrow confines of the hillbilly record buying market.

In a 1953 article, Hank Snow and Ernest Tubb (two singers who have been particularly influenced by Rodgers) suggested that

> He made it possible for cowboy or country singers to get employment on radio stations. He was responsible for the sale of more guitars than any other man. He made the value of country songs and records into a commercial product that since then has been recognised as an important part of the music industry. He made

it possible for hillbilly entertainers to play theatres and first rate entertainment places.[13]

Tubb and Snow overestimate Rodgers' importance in radio, for hillbilly performers had been featured on the air long before the Singing Brakeman. But, in the main, their comments hold true. We would suggest that Rodgers' influence on the development of country music was twofold. First, he made the recording companies and the entertainment media aware of the vast untapped wealth of country musicians, and perhaps even more significantly, of the vast potential audience for country music — providing it was served up in the prescribed manner. Secondly, more than any other individual artist, Jimmie Rodgers was responsible for a performing style and repertoire that were to dominate the country music market well into the '40s and '50s, and are still discernable today in the style of many major performers. As Malone has suggested:

> In assessing Jimmie Rodgers' influence on American folk music and on a later generation of commercial performers, one can safely use the adjective 'phenomenal'. Indeed, one would be hard pressed to find a performer in the whole broad field of 'pop' music — whether it be Al Jolson, Bing Crosby, or Frank Sinatra — who has exerted a more profound and recognizable influence on later generations of entertainers.[14]

Ernest Tubb has suggested that 75% of contemporary American country singers have been directly influenced by the Rodgers style;[15] and while researching in Australia, John Greenway came to the conclusion that 'all contemporary country singing is clearly attributable to Rodgers' compositions, themes and styles'.[16]

From the time of his initial success, Rodgers-style singers flooded the recording studios; and for many devotees, the personification of hillbilly music was the yodelling singer. Before beginning a discussion of some of these performers, it is worth pointing out that the majority of Rodgers' followers had less traditional repertoires than earlier country musicians and many, in fact, wrote their own songs. The whole emphasis of the country music repertoire was shifting from traditional songs to contemporary compositions. It is no exaggeration to say that the current repertoire of country music, the Nashville Sound, leans heavily towards love songs and ballads — perhaps as much as 75–80% of all recorded songs. It seems to us that this trend began with Jimmie Rodgers.

Interestingly, Rodgers' style even extended into the labour movement's musical activities. Ella May Wiggins, the martyred North Carolina strike leader, used *Waiting for a Train* as the basis of her protest song *All Around the Jailhouse*. Unfortunately Ella May was never recorded, but the text of the song remains. *Daddy and Home* was used by Sarah Ogan Gunning for her anti-capitalist manifesto *I'm Thinking Tonight of an Old Southern Town:*

I'm thinking tonight of an old southern town,
And the loved ones that I left behind,
I know they are naked and hungry too,
And it sure does worry my mind.

(Sarah Ogan Gunning, Folk-Legacy FSA-26)

Before his death, his popularity was manifested by the many singers who began to record in his style. Some were already well-known performers like Carson Robison, who recorded *My Carolina Sunshine Girl.* Others were traditional stringband musicians such as John Foster (of Rutherford and Foster) who recorded *Blue Yodel No. 5* and *Dear Old Sunny South By The Sea* for Gennett. But mostly they were young men, avid fans of Rodgers' style, who were inspired to record in a similar manner. Even as early as 1930, Gene Autry, Cliff Carlisle and Bill Cox had recorded many cover versions of Jimmie's songs as well as a considerable number of their own songs written in the Rodgers style. Probably the singers who came closest to Jimmie's style were those who remained virtually unknown; the Gennett recordings by Howard Keesee and the rare Okeh sides by Bill Bruner, for example. As they came so close to Rodgers' style, it is easy to see why they remained unknown. String bands rarely recorded Rodgers' songs, and some major performers purposely avoided the style. Tex Ritter, whose career also began in 1927, bought Jimmie's records but confessed that 'As everyone seemed to be doing yodelling songs or event songs I thought I'd keep clear of them'.[17]

Even women singers were influenced by Rodgers. Patsy Montana, 'The Cowboy's Sweetheart', won first prize in a 1931 talent contest by singing two of Jimmie's songs. She later embarked on a successful recording career. Still active in music today, Patsy has expressed interest in recording an album of Rodgers' compositions.[18] One wonders how many other singers began their careers under the same influence. Many artists such as Red Foley, Elton Britt, T. Texas Tyler and Tommy Duncan have named Rodgers as their inspiration, but although they recorded yodels on early performances, they did not record Jimmie's songs until they had established themselves. Others, such as Dwight Butcher, Daddy John Love, Fred Kirby, Leon Huff, Jesse Rogers and many more began as Rodgers devotees. Jerry Behrens labelled himself as 'Louisiana's Blue Yodeller' and Frankie Marvin had records credited to 'Oklahoma's Blue Yodeller'. The years since Jimmie's death have seen many more singers influenced by him: Bill Monroe, Slim Clarke, Rex Griffin, even singers who are generally considered more as members of the 'folk scene', such as Woody Guthrie, who even recorded his own version of a blue yodel:

Opposite: *some of the artists inspired by Jimmie Rodgers. Top, Kentuckians Jimmie Skinner* (left) *and Bill Carlisle. Bottom, Patsy Montana, Lefty Frizzell. Skinner, Carlisle and Montana are all still active in music; Frizzell died in 1975.*

I got the dust pneumonee, pneumonee in my lung,
And I ain't got long, not long.

Guthrie cleverly gets around his inability to yodel with the following verse,

There ought to be some yodelling in this song,
But I can't yodel, I got the dust pneumonee in my lungs.
(Woody Guthrie, *Dust Pneumonia Blues,* RCA LPV-502)

To some extent, this was fostered by the record companies, for once Rodgers was recognised as a hot commercial property, those companies were quick to seek performers in the Rodgers style. In some ways this was dictated by economic necessity for in the Depression years many record companies were faced with the choice of cutting expenses or closing down.

Thus it was cheaper to record a solo performer than a four-piece band. True, Jimmie Rodgers was always provided with lavish accompaniments, but his records were guaranteed good sales. This argument is supported by what happened to Kelly Harrell, composer of Rodgers' first hit. Harrell never played an instrument himself but relied on others. In 1929, Victor offered him the choice of learning an instrument and providing his own backing or hiring musicians out of his own fees. Harrell chose to retire from recording. But the fact was that Victor had decided that his sales were not sufficient to justify the expense of his stringband backing. [19]

We have mentioned many singers who followed the Rodgers style but to mention them all would require a substantial lengthening of this book. Here, however, we must discuss two who, because of their longevity within the country music industry and their devotion to Jimmie Rodgers, deserve closer attention. These are Ernest Tubb and Hank Snow. Tubb, although he never met Rodgers, may, as Malone has pointed out, be considered his protegé because of the help and encouragement given him by Carrie Rodgers. [20]

Tubb was born in 1914, in Crisp, Texas. By the age of 13 he was a confirmed Rodgers addict. His family moved to San Antonio during the time that Rodgers was resident there, but Tubb was never to meet Jimmie. He modelled his style completely on Rodgers', and reputedly knew every note of every song Jimmie had written. After he had decided to become a singer his career was given a boost when he persuaded Carrie Rodgers to listen to him on station KONO. Carrie lent him one of Jimmie's guitars and arranged a theatre tour for him. Ironically, it was not until he gave up singing in the Rodgers style that he found any success. After a brief flirtation with Victor, Tubb signed with Decca in 1940 and eventually become one of their most successful artists. He has remained amazingly loyal to the memory of Jimmie Rodgers, although today there is little influence evident in his own performing style. But Ernest Tubb has had a considerable influence on the development of country music. He was one of the first hillbilly performers to feature an electric guitar in his band. He was also influential in spreading the 'western' image in country music. It was Tubb who first introduced western clothes to the Grand Ole Opry in 1942. He was elected to the Country Music Hall of Fame in 1965, only four years after its foundation and the election of his idol Jimmie Rodgers.

As with Ernest Tubb, it was the Rodgers influence that made Clarence 'Hank' Snow seek a career in music. Snow was born in Nova Scotia. After a short time in the merchant navy he turned to music, and in 1936 he secured a contract with Victor in Montreal. His early recordings included many of his own compositions but also a sizeable proportion of Jimmie's songs. Snow was first billed as the 'Yodelling Ranger' and presented a strong western image by appearing with his trained horse Pawnee. As his voice deepened, his yodelling ability vanished. Undeterred, Hank billed himself as the 'Singing Ranger' and won even greater acclaim with his

Hank Snow and Ernest Tubb with Rodgers' guitar.

patriotic songs during World War II. After a temporary lull in his career in the late '40s, Snow has gone on to become one of country music's best known performers. Unlike Tubb, Hank Snow still retains many of Jimmie Rodgers' songs in his repertoire. Interestingly, Snow is one of the few singers who has carried on the Rodgers tradition of train songs. He even christened his son Jimmie Rodgers Snow. Although his later recordings feature electric instruments and current Nashville trends, Snow has probably stayed closer to the Rodgers style than any other major singer in the country style.

Strangely, the Rodgers influence was even felt in England. Harry Torrani was one singer who was influenced to some degree by Rodgers. First recorded in 1931, he featured many songs in the Rodgers style. In Australia, Tex Morton, 'The Yodelling Boundary Rider', may be said to have been the first Rodgers follower. From the beginning of his career in 1936/7, Morton's guitar style, vocals and repertoire were all heavily influenced by Rodgers, though his yodelling owes more to the unusual style of Goebel Reeves. As John Greenway has suggested, the Rodgers influence is common in modern Australian styles. Even in England today,

Above, *Harry Torrani, English yodeller, and Hank Snow.* Opposite, *Jesse Rodgers in the '30s.*

Brian Golbey, voted the top country music artist in 1972, drew his original inspiration from his father's collection of Jimmie Rodgers records.

Ironically, the man who had the best claim to be Jimmie's successor was fated to meet with little success in his life and career. This was Jesse Rodgers — Jimmie's cousin. Jesse began his recording career in March 1934, in San Antonio, when he cut four titles for Victor. His first recordings were very much in the Rodgers style — solo guitar accompaniment with runs, yodelling breaks, and a vocal style reminiscent of Jimmie's relaxed southern drawl. Some of Jesse's early titles are also in the familiar Rodgers style: *Way Down in Mississippi, Rambler's Yodel, When the Texas Moon is Shining* and *Yodelling the Railroad Blues.* However, Jesse recorded only one of Jimmie's songs. *Why Did You Give Me Your Love* which he retitled *Give Me Your Love.* Although this is from Jimmie's recording, Jesse adds a spoken commentary in the middle of the song. When Jimmie's recording of *My Good Gal's Gone Blues* was finally issued in 1936, a Jesse Rodgers song, *Leave Me Alone Sweet Mama,* was on the reverse. Possibly this was an error on the part of Victor and they mistook Jesse's recording for another title by Jimmie; or perhaps it was a publicity gimmick to introduce Jimmie's successor to the public. Bearing in mind the similarity of names and singing styles, and Jesse's claim that he came from Mississippi, many collectors began to wonder if there was not some family connection between the two men. Finally, in the early '50s, the late John Edwards contacted Carrie Rodgers about this. She replied that Jesse was Jimmie's half-cousin. However, this relationship was unconfirmed until recently and many experts held conflicting opinions, and Jesse himself confused the issue in a 1950 interview.

A brief article, based upon an interview with Jesse, appeared in the October 1950 issue of *Country Song Roundup.* Here, Jesse did not claim any family relationship with Jimmie but did say that his (Jesse's) mother raised Jimmie. Jimmie would watch Jesse practising and once,

> When I had done one of Maw's favourites called *Short Life of Trouble*, I meandered into one of my own compositions called *Sleep, Baby, Sleep*, and when I finished, Jimmy [*sic*] advised me to keep at it.[22]

Because of several dubious statements in the article the whole piece is suspect. If Jesse is referring to the standard *Sleep, Baby, Sleep*, it was obviously not his composition. Photographs of Jesse taken in the '50s show him to be a remarkably young man, and it seems likely that his recording career began while he was still in his teens. Thus, it seems unlikely that his 'Maw' raised Jimmie. Further on in the article Jesse claimed his career began on a Meridian radio station. Yet enquiries by us there revealed that no one had ever heard of him — not even Jimmie's

half-brother Jake Smith. He had been related surely someone would have been able to confirm the relationship.

Jim Evans, president of the Jimmie Rodgers Society, in conversation with Nolan Porterfield, claimed that Jesse was 'a guy who had nearly the same name and tried to make the most of it'.[23] When Porterfield later raised the subject again, Evans 'confirmed that Jesse and Jimmie were cousins of some sort'.[24] Prynce Wheeler, vice-president of the society, told us that he had last met Jesse in 1957, and that he believed his given name was Otto.[25] However, further enquiries revealed nothing about an Otto Rodgers. Eventually, in correspondence with Anita Rodgers Court, we discovered Jesse's whereabouts only to find that he had already died. However, with the kind help of Irene Lemon, Jesse's nurse, and a booklet prepared by Jimmie Otto Rodgers, Jesse's son, we have been able to gather Jesse's relationship with Jimmie and piece together his story.

Jesse Otto Rodgers was born in Waynesboro, Mississippi in 1911. His father, F. G. Rodgers, was Aaron's brother. In 1923, Jesse's mother died and he was sent to live with relatives in southwest Texas. Around 1932 he decided to become a full-time musician, no doubt inspired by Jimmie's example. He began his career with stations XERA, XEPN and XELO, powerful Mexican border stations. It seems possible that he worked with Jimmie at Texas appearances in 1932, but we lack confirmation of this. His Jimmie Rodgers-styled recordings lasted only until the late '30s and from that time on he began to develop a strong western image. His recordings after the war were almost exclusively cowboy style – *Riding Down the Canyon, Back in the Saddle Again,* and *The Cowboy's Heaven* are typical examples. Jesse worked for many years from Philadelphia and in 1949 took part in the first live TV western, 'The Western Balladeer'. This was followed by his own TV show 'Ranger Joe'.

As an old time artist, Jesse had never received the attention due to him, and now, on the verge of stardom with his western image, he was struck by misfortune. In 1960 it was discovered that he was suffering from emphysema, a destructive lung disease. By 1963 the disease had curtailed his musical activities and forced him into retirement. From then until his death in December 1973, Jesse sustained himself by writing songs and western stories. It seems a great pity that none of Jesse's early recordings have been reissued for many are fine examples of the blue yodel. Although these early recordings are very much in the Jimmie Rodgers style, it would be unfair to accuse Jesse of trying to cash in on his cousin's popularity, and it would seem that Jesse probably deliberately avoided recording Jimmie's material.

Throughout this chapter we have made frequent mention of Jim Evans and in view of his contribution to the memory of Jimmie Rodgers, his

Opposite, top, *the masthead of the magazine* Blue Yodeler, *and,* bottom, *membership card of the fanclub.*

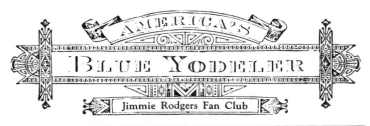

VOL. 2   SPRING JOURNAL - 1954   **NO. 2**

work should be examined here. Evans, of Lubbock, Texas, first heard Jimmie's records in the late '30s. At first he had aspirations to be a singer himself, but a tonsillectomy ended his yodelling ability. In 1938 he began systematically to collect Jimmie's recordings and any memorabilia pertaining to the singer. Through his massive correspondence with other Rodgers collectors, Evans eventually built up a complete set of Jimmie's records. However, both he and his correspondents felt that there was a need for a Jimmie Rodgers fan club. This finally became a reality in 1947 with Evans as president and Carrie Rodgers as honorary president. The winter of 1952 saw the publication of its journal *The Blue Yodeler,* an informative little magazine which ran for six issues. However, failing health and other pressures forced Evans to cease publication in 1954. This was followed by occasional newsletters until 1963, when ill-health and other personal setbacks forced Evans to give up his work. No one can possibly doubt Evans' obvious admiration (even adulation) of Jimmie Rodgers, nor can the amazing progress that he made in many ways be minimised. Certainly the club enabled many collectors to build or complete their Rodgers sets; and it seems likely that the early album reissues by Victor

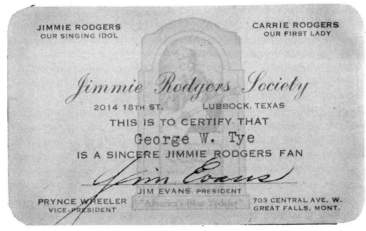

would never have been made available without the club's active campaign. Also, *The Blue Yodeler* frequently contained little-known aspects of historical importance. The only criticism we would make of Jim Evans was that he revealed only certain material from his vast collection — material which in many cases had been given him by fellow enthusiasts on the understanding that it would eventually be used for publication in *The Blue Yodeler* or in newsletters. However, it seems that Evans felt himself to be some kind of censor, suppressing anything which he felt was not in keeping with his conception of Rodgers. Nevertheless, it was the activities of Evans and his club, with Hank Snow and Ernest Tubb, that eventually resulted in the first 'Jimmie Rodgers Memorial Day' in Meridian in 1953.

Through the efforts of Rodgers' fans and many country musicians, a powerful movement emerged in the early '50s to erect some lasting monument to Jimmie Rodgers. The most suitable location for this was thought to be Meridian, Mississippi. The movement, spearheaded by Hank Snow, Ernest Tubb, Carrie Rodgers and Jim Evans, was well under way in the summer of 1952. At that time, Snow and Tubb visited the city for preliminary discussions. At the same time Jasper H. Skewes, owner of the Meridian *Star,* was also planning to dedicate a monument to the city's railroad men. Realising Jimmie's close association with the railroad, a double ceremony was eventually organised for 26 May 1953. Both parties were considerably helped by the Meridian Chamber of Commerce, which obviously realised the enormous commercial benefits of such a venture. The attendance at the Memorial Day was amazing by any standard and a vast crowd of Rodgers' fans and country enthusiasts packed the city. Even the Mandrake and Flash Gordon strip cartoons in the Meridian *Star* were enlisted in the publicity campaign.

A monument dedicated to Jimmie's memory was unveiled by Ernest Tubb; and a steam locomotive, donated by the Meridian and Bigbee

Railroad, was dedicated to the railroad men. With the Rodgers monument were two plaques, one dedicated by Ralph Peer and one by RCA-Victor. Naturally, many stars of country music were present at the dedications. The state governors of Mississippi and Tennessee were present, as was ex-governor Jimmie Davis of Louisiana. (The politicians used the occasion

Illustrations on pp. 154-7: *the Jimmie Rodgers Memorial Day*. Below, this page, *the monument, flanked by the Snows and the Tubbs*.

for a little campaigning, to which many of those present strongly objected.) The whole day had a carnival quality with a parade, floats, and a star-studded evening concert. The local cinema ran continuous performances of Jimmie's film *The Singing Brakeman*. Tubb, Snow, Lefty Frizzell, Cowboy Copas, Bill Monroe, Roy Acuff and The Carter Family performed at the evening concert. So did Ian Lee, a sixteen-year-old English boy who had been sponsored by Meridian businessmen. Lee was presented with a cowboy outfit by Tubb and was interviewed on local

Top, *the Memorial Day of 1954: Sen. Nate Williamson, Anita Rodgers, Carrie Rodgers, Lottie Mae Mixon. (Nate Williamson was one of Carrie's brothers.)* Bottom, *the English Rodgers devotee Ian Lee, who attended the 1953 ceremony.*

radio. One of the highlights of the concert was Bill Bruner's performance of *My Old Pal,* which he dedicated to Carrie Rodgers. After the performance, he presented the guitar which Jimmie had given him to Jimmie Rodgers Snow, Hank's son.

Above, *Hank Snow, his son Jimmie Rodgers Snow (with the Rodgers guitar given him by Bill Bruner) and Don Owens.* Opposite, *the 1954 Memorial Day.* Top, *guests Adlai Stevenson and State Governor Hugh White drive through the Meridian streets.* Centre, *Ernest Tubb, Carrie Rodgers, Jim Evans, Hank Snow, Jimmie Rodgers Snow.* Bottom, *one of the floats in the parade.*

1954 saw, if anything, an even more successful Memorial Day, with Adlai Stevenson in attendance. Eventually, the interested parties began campaigning for a 'National Hillbilly Day', but many of Meridian's citizens objected to the city being labelled a hillbilly town, The Meridian Memorial Day's popularity has declined somewhat, no doubt because of the increasing importance of Nashville as the Country Music Capital, but the Rodgers Day still sporadically takes place.

At the early celebrations, Carrie Rodgers was a highly honoured guest. After Jimmie's death, Carrie took great interest in the development of country music and was a well-loved and respected figure. Many well-known singers owe their success to her efforts, and she worked tirelessly to further Jimmie's memory. In 1956, a nostalgic reunion took place between Carrie Rodgers and The Carter Family. A recording session was arranged by Acme Records and Cliff Spurlock, the Carters' recording manager. The issued title *Mrs Jimmie Rodgers Visits the Carter Family* (Acme 1010) is similar in format to the recording by Jimmie and the Carters. Maybelle Carter was not present on the recording but A.P.'s

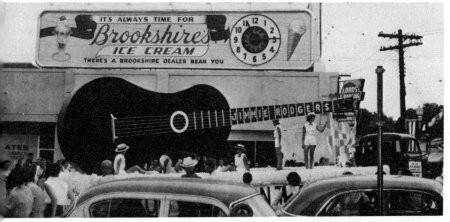

children Joe and Janette can be heard. The recording was made in Bristol. As Carrie recalled,

> April 20, 1956 was the never-to-be forgotten day the Carter Family and I answered the requests of many of you who have written thru' the years, asking that we get together for a visit on record — like the Carters and Jimmie did so long ago . . .
>
> Our 'trip' could almost be called a parade, for the entire group walked from the hotel carrying instruments down State Street just as the Carters and Jimmie had done on that memorable occasion in August of '28 [sic] — to the very same old brick building where they had auditioned and made their first records . . .
>
> You can imagine the mixed emotions we had on this occasion. Joy and laughter — sadness and tears — and pride — all mingled together as the years seemed to roll away . . . Joy at being together, sadness for the one missing — My Jimmie.[26]

During her last years, Carrie's ambition was to see a film version of her husband's life. Several companies were interested; and to finalise the film she spent much of 1959 in Hollywood conferring with writers and producers. She even completed a screenplay. However, the option expired in 1960 and the project was shelved. Many people assumed that Jimmie's great success had meant that he left a fortune, but this was far from true. During the last two years of his life, his medical costs had consumed the greater part of his income. After his death, his royalty payments provided only for Carrie and Anita's living expenses. When Carrie was discovered to be suffering from cancer, Jim Evans launched an appeal to country music enthusiasts to pay her hospital costs. Despite extensive surgery, Carrie Rodgers died on 28 November 1961.

In 1955, Jimmie's own recordings, which had been more or less continually available since their original issue, received a boost. Victor decided to 'update' some of his best sellers. On 18 March, at the Nashville studios, a bizarre session was arranged. The resulting recordings were

Mrs Jimmie Rodgers (centre) *with the Carter Family, 1956: Joe, Sara, Janette, A.P.*

credited to 'Jimmie Rodgers with the Rainbow Ranch Boys' and consisted of a group of eminent musicians dubbed on to Rodgers' original masters. As the group use the name of Hank Snow's backing group, one wonders how much Snow had to do with arranging this session. Eight titles were used in the dubbing operation, and the musicians involved were Chet Atkins (guitar), Joe Talbot (steel guitar), Tommy Vaden (fiddle) and Ernie Newton (bass).

The four musicians added a tasteful backing to four titles: *In the Jailhouse Now, Muleskinner Blues, Peach Picking Time in Georgia* and *Mother, Queen of My Heart*. Of these, *Jailhouse* proved extremely popular and even reached the Billboard C&W charts. *Peach Picking* and *Mother* sound a shade peculiar as they already had fiddle, banjo and guitar accompaniment. *Muleskinner Blues* is more interesting, but the careful listener will note that Jimmie's original guitar solo in the middle of the song is cut short. Could it be that Chet Atkins was not able to follow the Rodgers runs, or was it that the surface noise on the original master necessitated a cut? One will never know, but it is interesting to note that that particular Rodgers run has never been duplicated by another artist on a recorded preformance.

On 22 July, the same musicians dubbed accompaniments to four more Rodgers masters. *Blue Yodel No. 1* and *Memphis Yodel* remain unissued, and the other two titles, *Never No Mo' Blues* and *Daddy and Home,* were only issued on a 45 rpm single in the States, now rare. Of the two titles, *Daddy and Home* is by far the more interesting. As a solo guitar item it cannot be counted amongst Jimmie's best recordings (even though it proved a commercial success over the years). However, with the Rainbow Ranch Boys' tasteful accompaniment the song is given a new lease of life.

Yet amongst the modernising of Jimmie's records, the ballyhoo and commercialism of the Meridian Memorial Day Festival, there is an amazing tribute to the Brakeman's popularity. It would be incorrect to assume that all those who attended Meridian were elderly, for Rodgers has found fans from successive generations all over the world. His LP reissues, first on 10" and then 12" albums, have all sold in excess of 30,000 copies within one year of their release in the US; and this surprising figure takes no account of sales overseas.[27] In Japan, Victor have issued a boxed set of all Jimmie's recordings complete with the Victor tribute album 'When Evening Shadows Fall'. In Britain RCA have issued two double albums. All this testifies to a wide and receptive audience for his music. Nor is his influence only present in the work of his surviving near-contemporaries such as Snow and Tubb. A surprising number of today's younger artists could be mentioned: among them Merle Haggard.

Haggard, a popular and commercially successful recording artist, who has explored many controversial and topical themes in his own writing, acknowledges a considerable debt to the music of Jimmie Rodgers. In 1969, Haggard recorded a double album of Jimmie's songs — an album which reveals a deep understanding of the man and his music. Interviewed in 1970 by Alice Foster, he said of the album ('Same Train, Different Time' [Capitol SWBB223]):

> I didn't put it out with the idea of selling it. I didn't even think it would sell. I put it out more or less for myself. I did it because I like Jimmie's records so much that I just enjoyed it. I wanted to do something that I could remember. It was for my family and people that I knew when I was a kid that used to sing all these Jimmie Rodgers songs.[28]

Jack Elliott is another second-generation singer who shows evidence of the Rodgers influence. Although better known for his interpretations of Woody Guthrie's songs, Elliott often includes a Rodgers song in his act. Jack even recorded a tribute album to Rodgers in England early in his career. As we write this chapter, a newly issued album from Maria Muldaur includes Jimmie's *Any Old Time*: a version which follows the original remarkably closely, and has the added interest of being one of the few Rodgers songs recorded by a woman.

Nor should it be thought that Jimmie Rodgers' influence was only confined to white hillbilly musicians. Enough evidence can be found to suggest that Rodgers was popular, if not influential, among black musicians. Naturally, his influence on these was nowhere near as dynamic as it was on white country musicians, but it does suggest a popularity which crossed, and recrossed, the colour line. Dave Evans, to whose research we have already referred, has commented on this:

> Black and white folk musicians in the American South have a long history of musical interchange . . . Yet by and large I have found in my field experience that black musicians show little interest in hillbilly and country and western records and their performers . . . The one white commercial recording artist who was an outstanding exception to this pattern was Jimmie Rodgers. He is well remembered by black musicians today, many of whom still perform some of his songs learned from records made some forty years ago.[30]

Eli Owens of Bogalusa, Louisiana, learned songs from Jimmie's records and still performs a version of *Blue Yodel No. 8*; and one could quote several more prominent blues musicians who learned from Rodgers either in person or from his records — John Jackson of Virginia, and Skip James and Mississippi John Hurt of Mississippi, for example. Bill Williams, a country bluesman from Virginia, remembered his brother buying Jimmie Rodgers' records from mail-order houses in the 1930s. When asked what records he particularly liked, he replied,

> Well, I'll tell the truth about it. My brother, he ordered these records and I really didn't know anything about who was on the records until they got there. But as far as playing music and singing, I'd rather listen to Jimmie Rodgers and how he used to play them songs as soon as anybody else I've ever heard. I liked his songs – he had a lovely voice!
>
> Did you ever try to do that yourself – that kind of yodel?
>
> Yodel? Yeah, I used to yodel, yeah.[31]

But is is difficult to assess Rodgers' influence on black song with any degree of accuracy because he had been so influenced by black song himself. We have briefly mentioned black influences which were at work on Jimmie during his formative years, and it is now time to make a closer examination of this.

Nolan Porterfield has pointed out that, because of its diversity, Rodgers' repertoire eludes any attempt to categorise it along strict lines of subject-matter or style. However, three broad genres seem to dominate: blues, railroad songs and love ballads — the remainder must be delegated to a catch-all which might be termed 'novelty' and would include such items as *Everybody Does It in Hawaii,* and *A Drunkard's Child,* the four cowboy songs, and the popular and sentimental items. However, the largest of these categories and, we would suggest, the most important, is the 13 blue yodels and the 25 related blues pieces. Without dismissing the remainder of his recorded repertoire, we feel that Rodgers' main contribution to

American music was the blending of traditional black blues stanzas and styles with his own creation, the blue yodel, and the resulting white blues style.

It is obvious that Rodgers' blues material is within the standard blues format. His accompaniment and vocal style is less fluid than most black artists, but lyrically Jimmie was considerably influenced by black song. But to attempt to discover if Rodgers was influenced by any one or two particular black singers would be foolish; for as Nolan Porterfield has said,

> It seems to me that much of the material drawn upon by both Rodgers and various black artists simply derives from common sources, as so much lyrical gruel floating in the community soup. In

some cases Rodgers seems to have picked it up first, in others he was borrowing from material already recorded.[32]

A few examples will clearly demonstrate this interaction: and here we gratefully acknowledge the work of Nolan Porterfield and Paul Oliver.

In 1929, Jimmie Rodgers recorded,

> When a woman gets the blues, she hangs her head and cries;
> But when a man gets the blues, he grabs a train and rides.
>
> (*Train Whistle Blues*, Victor 22379)

Two years later, Peetie Wheatstraw the blues artist employed the same verse, modifying the last line to 'He flags a freight train and rides' (*C. and A. Blues*, Vocalion 04592). Jimmie's *Blue Yodel No. 9* of 1930 uses

> Standing on the corner, I didn't mean no harm,
> Along come a police, he took me by the arm.
>
> (*Blue Yodel No. 9*, Victor 23580)

While the black Jimmie Gordon used the following variation in his *Number Runner's Blues* recorded in 1938:

> Standing on the corner, I didn't mean no harm,
> Ooh, that policeman was looking, he grabbed me by the arm.
>
> (*Number Runner's Blues*, Decca 7536)

In *Blue Yodel No. 8* Jimmie used

> I like to work, I'm rolling all the time,
> I can pop my initials on a mule's behind.
>
> (*Blue Yodel No. 8*, Victor 23503)

While from a 1935 Leadbelly recording we have,

> Honey I'm down in the bottom's, skinnin' for Johnny Ryan,
> Puttin' my initials, honey, on a mule's behind.
>
> (*Honey, I'm All Out and Down*, Melotone 13326)

And Jimmie's borrowings are equally evident. In 1923, Ma Rainey recorded,

> If your house catch a-fire and there ain't no water round,
> Throw your stuff out the window, and let that shack burn down.
>
> (*Southern Blues*, Paramount 12083)

Rodgers altered the verse only slightly when he recorded it in the *Brakeman's Blues* of 1928. The same year he sang,

> I'm going to the river, take me a rocking chair,
> And if the blues don't leave me, I'll rock on away from here.
>
> (*Memphis Yodel*, Victor 21636)

— a verse which had appeared with only slight variations in Sadie McKinney's 1927 recording of *Rock Away Blues* (Victor 20565). The interaction of lyrics is equally shown in a comparison of phrases Rodgers shared with black singers: 'good gal', 'ride the blinds', 'sweet loving daddy', 'whole round world' and many, many more.

Paul Oliver has examined the significance of sexual imagery in the blues;[33] and in this discussion of interaction between Jimmie Rodgers and black musicians the topic is an important one. In the vein of sexual symbols, Jimmie was following black precedents when he used phrases such as 'jelly roll', 'peaches', 'damper', 'grinding', 'switching', 'hauling your ashes' and 'rocking', for they were all established and well-known expressions for sexual intercourse within the blues form. For example, Rodgers used,

> I smell your bread a-burning, turn your damper down,
> If you ain't got no damper, good gal, turn yo' bread around.
> > (*Blue Yodel No. 8*, Victor 23503)

and

> When you see a spider climbing up a wall,
> You can tell the world he's gonna get his ashes hauled.
> > (*Let Me Be Your Sidetrack*, Victor 23621)

Similarly, his line

> Ground hog rootin' in my back yard at night
> > (*Blue Yodel No. 10*, Victor 23696)

occurs in several blues by black singers:

> Mama, can't you hear this tush hog rootin' round your backdoor?
> > (Bo Carter, *Tush Hog Blues*, Bluebird B-8514)

and from Big Joe Williams

> I'm a rootin' ground hog, babe, I roots everywhere I go.
> > (*Rootin' Ground Hog Blues*, Bluebird B-7065)

The established admiration amongst blacks for large women is also evident in Jimmie's recordings.

> She's long, she's tall, she's six feet from the ground.
> > (*Blue Yodel No. 3*, Victor 21531)

> I don't want no skinny mama, I want one with plenty of meat.
> > (*Looking For A New Mama*, Victor 23580)

While from black singers there are numerous verses similar to

> I got a big, fat woman, grease shaking on her bone.
> > (Blind Boy Fuller, *I'm A Good Stem Winder*, Vocalion 04137)

While references to women with 'great big legs' in the blues could be listed until the end of this chapter.

It would be incorrect for us to convey the impression that Rodgers was the first white blues singer, for one could cite many white performers who recorded before Jimmie's debut in 1927. Some of these came much closer to the black sound. Frank Hutchison, for example, who also had a more authentic style of guitar playing; or the incredible vocal style of Dock

Boggs, the Virginia miner and banjoist. After Rodgers' appearance, there were Dick Justice and Larry Hensley, to quote only two examples of white musicians who sounded far 'blacker' than he did. However, we would suggest that Rodgers was important in two respects. Firstly, he was a legitimate interpreter of the blues form; and secondly, he reached a far wider audience than any other blues artist — black or white. Thus, as he took the blues form with him to this audience, it seems to us that he was influential in popularising the blues among white audiences, and may well have contributed to making black blues an acceptable branch of American folkmusic. The late Kenneth Allsop has suggested that Rodgers' work was a

> polite devitalization — nothing more disturbing than wistful sentimentality — of the harsh, despairing blues he must have heard in the South.[34]

We hope that the above examples will show that Allsop's criticism was somewhat unjustified, even though Jimmie's blues material was mainly confined to the risqué style of the 'good time blues'.

The remainder of Rodgers' recorded repertoire (i.e that part which does not come into the blues category) has been dismissed as of 'little interest to folklorists' by John Greenway.[35] Yet it is clearly evident that the folk themselves were, and still are, interested in this material. And here it seems a case of the folklorist telling the folk what they should like. Certainly, the basis for the bulk of Rodgers' recorded repertoire came from folk sources: was reshaped, given back to the folk, and later recollected by folklorists. But as Malone points out, 'only Vance Randolph mentions Rodgers' name'[36] — even though his songs are listed in the Library of Congress checklists and in the published compilations of a number of folklorists.

When Jimmie Rodgers died in 1933, the first decade of commercial country music died with him. But by that time hillbilly music was firmly attached to the entertainment industry and, in future, would be moulded by the same influences which shape any other form of popular music: a transformation which Jimmie Rodgers was instrumental in creating. Today, in the electronic age of country music, the influence of the Singing Brakeman is still evident. Jimmie Rodgers may be dead, but his music is still very much alive.

Another commemoration: in the Country Music Wax Museum, Nashville.

8/The Jimmie Rodgers Discography

This Discography includes details of all known takes of Jimmie Rodgers' recordings, whether issued or unissued. For easy reference, issued takes are denoted by the song-titles appearing in bold type. Superscript numbers refer to notes, which may be found in their place after the notes to the preceding chapters. Standard discographical abbreviations are used for record-labels, the more important of these being explained below. In the column of record issues at the right-hand side of the Discography, all entries up to the semicolon are 78 rpm issues, and all following it are EP/LP issues. Where no semicolon appears, all the entries belong to one of these categories. It will be clear, from the abbreviations used, which category applies.

The names in italics and parentheses following the song-titles are the composer/s as credited on the original record-labels (though they did not necessarily appear on all such issues).

Abbreviations

Except where noted otherwise, all serials or prefixes refer to US issues, and all are 78 rpm pressings.

Vi	=	VICTOR (RCA Victor) 20000/21000/22000/23000/24000, V-40000,21-0000,18-6000 (Picture Record),27-0000,420-0000/447-0000; P/PT (78 rpm album); EPA, EPAT, WPT (EP); LPT (10" LP); LPM, LSP (12" LP); DPL, VPS (double LP). *Britain:* RCX (EP); RD (LP); DPM/DPS (double LP). *Australia:* (A) EP (EP); L (LP). *Japan:* JA, A; HP (10" LP), AP, RA, SRA (12" LP).
Bb	=	BLUEBIRD B-5000/6000/7000, 33-0500.
MW	=	MONTGOMERY WARD M-3000/4000/5000/8000.
El	=	ELECTRADISK 1800/1900/2000.
Su	=	SUNRISE S-3000.
Co	=	COLUMBIA *Ireland:* IFB. *France:* MZ.

HMV = HIS MASTER'S VOICE   *Britain:* MH; 7EG (EP). *Australia:* EA. *India:* N.

Zo = ZONOPHONE   *Britain:* 4000/5000/6000, T5000/6000. *Australia:* T5000/6000, EE.

RZ = REGAL ZONOPHONE   *Britain:* ME, MR. *Ireland:* IZ. *Australia:* G. *India:* MR20000.

[*Note: the Zonophone label was amalgamated with the British Regal label in mid-1933 to become Regal Zonophone. The green-label Zonophones in the 5000/6000 series were reissued on Regal Zonophone with a T prefix. Similarly, the Australian Zonophone EE releases were reissued with a Regal Zonophone label. All the British T-series items were issued in Australia with identical numbers, except where the coupling had already been released there with an EE number.*]

Tw = TWIN   *India:* FT.

CAL = CAMDEN (RCA Camden)   CAL (LP).

CMH = COUNTRY MUSIC HISTORY   *West Germany:* CMH (LP).

The authors acknowledge the assistance of the late John Edwards, George Tye, John Stoten, Brian Rust, Frank Mare, Nolan Porterfield, Masumi Tsuchiya and Robert E. Nobley.

Vocal (and yodelling*) with own guitar. 408 State St, Bristol, Tenn., August 4, 1927

39767-1,2,3	The Soldier's Sweetheart	Vi unissued
39767-4	**The Soldier's Sweetheart**	Vi 20864, MW M-4452,
	(Rodgers)	Bb 33-0513, HMV EA1400,
		RZ G23197; RD7505, LPM2531,
		RA5459, DPM2047, DPL2-0075
39768-1,2	*Sleep, Baby, Sleep	Vi unissued
39768-3	***Sleep, Baby, Sleep** *(–)*	Vi 20864, Bb B-6225,
		MW M-4452, HMV EA1400,
		RZ G23197, MR2795,
		Tw FT8585, Vi A1466,
		21-0180, 27-0104, P318; WPT23,
		EPAT23, LPT3038, LPM2213,
		RD27241, DPS2021, RA5176,
		RA5459, RA5510, RA9037

Camden, N.J., November 30, 1927

40751-1	Ben Dewberry's Final Run	Vi unissued
40751-2	**Ben Dewberry's Final Run**	Vi 21245, Bb B-5482,
	(Andrew Jenkins)	RZ G23117, MR2241, IZ495,
		Tw FT8185; LPM1640,
		RD27110, DPS2021, RA5459
40752-1	**Mother Was a Lady (If**	Vi 21433, Bb B-5482,
	Brother Jack Were Here)[1]	MW M-4224, HMV EA1382,
	(Edward B. Marks-Joseph	RZ G23193, MR2241, IZ495;
	W. Stern)	Tw FT1808; LPM2865, RD7644,
		RA5459
40752-2	Mother Was a Lady (If Brother	Vi unissued
	Jack Were Here)	
40753-1	*Blue Yodel	Vi unissued
40753-2	***Blue Yodel** *(Rodgers)*	Vi 21142, Bb B-5085, Su S-3172,
		MW M-3272, Zo 5158, RZ T5158,
		IZ310, Vi 21-0042, 27-0098,
		P244; WPT21, EPAT21, WPT6,
		LPT6, LPT3037, HMV 7EG8163,
		VPS6091
	Note: *on the following issues*	
	part of the guitar solo after	
	verse 4 is edited out:	EPA5097, RCX1058, LPM2112,
		(A)EP20219, L10883, LSP3315,
		RA5176, RA5459, RA5510,
		RA9037, DPM2047, DPL-2-0075
40754-1	Away Out on the Mountain	Vi unissued
40754-2	**Away Out on the Mountain**	Vi 21142, Bb B-5085, Su S-3172,
	(Kelly Harrell)	MW M-3272, Zo EE109, 5158,
		RZ T5158, IZ310, Tw FT1733
		Vi 21-0042, 27-0098, P244;
		WPT21, EPAT21, WPT6, LPT6,
		LPT3037, HMV 7EG8163,
		RCX1058, (A)EP20219,
		LPM2112, L10883, EPA5097,
		LSP3315, RA5459, RA5501,
		VPS6091, DPM2047, DPL2-0075

Vocal and yodelling with own ukulele. E.T. Cozzens (steel guitar, mandolin),
J.R. Ninde (guitar).[2]

Studio No. 1, Camden, N.J., February 14, 1928

41736-1	**Dear Old Sunny South by the Sea** *(J. Rodgers-E.T. Cozzens)*	Vi 21574, Bb B-6246, Zo 5341, RZ T5341, IZ317, G23188, HMV EA1228, N4336, Vi A1454, 21-0182, 27-0106, P318; WPT23, EPAT410, LPT3039, LPM1232, RD27138, RA5176, RA5459, RA5510, RA9037, VPS6091, DPM2047, DPL2-0075
41736-2	Dear Old Sunny South by the Sea	Vi unissued

Vocal and yodelling with E.T. Cozzens (steel guitar), J.R. Ninde (guitar).

41737-1	Treasures Untold	Vi unissued
41737-2	**Treasures Untold** *(J. Rodgers-E.T. Cozzens)*[3]	Vi 21433, Bb B-5838, MW M-4217, Zo EE139, HMV N4310, Tw FT9115; (A)EP20176, LPM1640, RD27110, DPS2021, VPS6091, RA5459, RA5510, RA5176

Vocal and yodelling with own guitar, E.T. Cozzens (ukulele).

41738-1	**The Brakeman's Blues** *(Rodgers)*	Vi 21291, MW M-4214, RZ G23116, HMV EA154?, N4364, Vi 21-0044, 27-0100, P244; WPT21, EPAT21, LPT3037, HMV 7EG8163, (A)EP20219, RCX1058, LPM2112, L10883, EPA5097, VPS6091, RA5459
41738-2	The Brakeman's Blues	Vi unissued

Vocal and yodelling with E.T. Cozzens (steel guitar), J.R. Ninde (guitar).

41739-1	**The Sailor's Plea** *(McWilliams-Rodgers)*	Vi V-40054, Bb B-6246, MW M-5036, Bb 33-0513, Zo 5401, IZ321, HMV N4327; LPM2531, RD7505, RA5459
41739-2	The Sailor's Plea	Vi unissued

Vocal and yodelling with own guitar, E. T. Cozzens (banjo).

Same location, February 15, 1928

41740-1	**In the Jailhouse Now** *(Rodgers)*	Vi 21245, Bb B-5223, El 2109, Su S-3306, Mw M-4721, Zo 4342, RZ G23202, HMV EA 1406, N4309; LPM2634, RD7562, VPS6091, RA5459, DPL2-0075
41740-2	In the Jailhouse Now	Vi unissued

Vocal and yodelling with own guitar, E. T. Cozzens (steel guitar).

41741-1	Blue Yodel No. 2	Vi unissued
41741-2	**Blue Yodel No. 2 (My Lovin' Gal, Lucille)** *(Rodgers)*	Vi 21291, MW M-4214, M-8121, Zo 4370, RZ G23116, MR3122, IZ1004, HMV EA1542, N4309, Tw FT8775, Vi A1454,[4] 21-0181, 27-0105, P318; WPT23, EPAT23, LPT3038, LPM2213, RD2741, DPS2021, RA5459

Vocal and yodelling with own guitar.

41742-1	Memphis Yodel	Vi unissued
41742-2	**Memphis Yodel** *(Rodgers)*	Vi 21636, MW M-4450, M-4725, Zo 5283, RZ T5283, IZ315, G23114, HMV EA1540, N4291; LPM2213, RD27241, DPS2021, RA5459
41743-1	Blue Yodel No. 3	Vi unissued
41743-2	**Blue Yodel No. 3** *(Rodgers)*	Vi 21531, MW M-4213, Zo 5247, RZ T5247, IZ314, Vi 21-0177, 27-0103, P282; WPT22, EPAT22, LPT3037, LPM2213, RD27241, DPS2021, RA5459

Vocal and yodelling with own guitar. Studio No. 1, Camden, N.J., June 12, 1928

45090-1	**My Old Pal** *(McWilliams-Rodgers)*	Vi 21757, Bb B-5609, Zo EE150, 5356, RZ T5356, IZ318, Tw FT1756, Vi 21-0176, 27-0102, P282; WPT22, EPAT22, LPT3037, LPM2213, RD27241, DPS2021, VPS6091, RA5460
45090-2	My Old Pal	Vi unissued
45091-1,2	Mississippi Moon	Vi unissued
45092	*unallocated*	
45093-1	**My Little Old Home Down in New Orleans** *(Rodgers)*[5]	Vi 21574, Bb B-5609, MW M-4218, Zo EE139, 5341, RZ T5341, IZ317, HMV N4336; LPM1640, RD27110, DPS2021, RA5460, DPL2-0075
45093-2	My Little Old Home Down in New Orleans	Vi unissued
45094-1	**You and My Old Guitar** *(McWilliams-Rodgers)*	Vi V-40072, Bb B-5083, El 2009, Su S-3170, MW M-4224, Zo 5423, RZ T5423, IZ323, Tw FT1276, Vi 420-0028, 447-0028; (A)EP21002, PT3035, EPAT411, LPT3039, LPM1232, RD27138, RA5460, DPM2047
45094-2	You and My Old Guitar	Vi unissued

(session continued over)

45095-1	**Daddy and Home** *(McWilliams-Rodgers)*	Vi 21757, Bb B-5991, MW M-8109, Zo EE150, 5356, RZ T5356, IZ318, Vi 21-0043, 27-0099, P244; WPT21, EPAT409, LPT3038, (A)EP21002, LPM1232, LSP3315, RD27138, VPS6091, RA5460
45095-2	Daddy and Home	Vi unissued
45096-1	**My Little Lady** *(McWilliams-Rodgers)*	Vi V-40072, Bb B-5838, MW M-4731, Zo 5423, RZ T5423, IZ323, HMV N4371, Vi 420-0029, 447-0029; PT3035, EPAT411, LPT3039
	Note: *On the following issues the first two notes are edited out:*	LPM1232, RD27138, RA5460, RA 5501
45096-2	My Little Lady	Vi unissued
45097-1,2	I'm Lonely And Blue	Vi unissued
45098-1	Lullaby Yodel	Vi unissued
45098-2	**Lullaby Yodel** *(McWilliams-Rodgers)*	Vi 21636, Bb B-5337, Su S-3418, MW M-4218, Zo 5283, RZ T5283, IZ315, G23114, HMV EA1540, N4291; LPM1640, RD27110, DPS2021, RA5460, RA5510, RA5176, RA9037
45099-1	**Never No Mo' Blues** *(Rodgers-McWilliams)*	Vi 21531, Bb B-6225, Zo EE109, 5247, RZ T5247, IZ314, Tw FT1733, Vi 21-0043, 27-0099, P244; WPT21, EPAT409, LPT3038, (A)EP21002, LPM1232, RD27138, VPS6091, RA5460, RA5510, RA5176
45099-2,3	Never No Mo' Blues	Vi unissued

Vocal and yodelling with C.L. Hutchison (cornet), James Rikard (clarinet), John Westbrook (steel guitar), Dean Bryan (guitar), George MacMillan (string bass).
Peachtree Rd, Atlanta, Ga., October 20, 1928

47215-1,2	My Carolina Sunshine Girl	Vi unissued
47215-3	**My Carolina Sunshine Girl** *(Rodgers)*	Vi V-40096, Bb B-5556, MW M-4451, Zo 5495, RZ T5495, HMV N4351, Vi 21-0180, 27-0104, P318; WPT23, EPAT23, LPT3038, RCX1058, (A)EP20219, LPM2112, L10883, EPA5097, VPS6091, RA5460, RA9037, DPM2047, DPL2-0075

47216-1,2,3	Blue Yodel No. 4	Vi unissued
47216-4	**Blue Yodel No. 4 (California Blues)** *(Rodgers)*	Vi V-40014, MW M-4722, M-8124, Zo 5380, RZ T5380, IZ320, HMV MH192, Vi 21-0175, 27-0101, P282; WPT22, EPAT409, LPT3038, LPM1232, RD27138, VPS6091, RA5460, RA9037

Vocal, yodelling and train-whistle effects with accompaniment as above.

Same location, October 22, 1928

47223- 1,2,3	Waiting For A Train	Vi unissued
47223-4	**Waiting For A Train**	Vi V-40014, HMV MH192
47223-4R	**Waiting For A Train** *(Rodgers)* [6]	Vi V-40014, Bb B-5163, El 2060, Su S-3244, MW M-8109, Zo 5380, RZ T5380, IZ320, Vi 21-0175, 27-0101, P282; WPT22, EPAT409, LPT3038, LPM1232, LSP3315, RD27138, VPS6091, RA5460, RA5501, HP526, AP3004, RA9037, DPL2-0075

Vocal and yodelling with C. L. Hutchison (cornet), John Westbrook (steel guitar), Dean Bryan (guitar), George MacMillan (string bass).

47224-1,2	I'm Lonely And Blue	Vi unissued
47224-3	**I'm Lonely And Blue**	Vi V-40054
47224-4	I'm Lonely And Blue	Vi unissued
47224-5R	**I'm Lonely And Blue** *(McWilliams-Rodgers)* [6]	Vi V-40054, MW M-4217, Zo 5401, RZ T5401, IZ321, HMV N4327; LPM2634, RD7562, RA5460

Vocal and yodelling with orchestra: unknown cornet, saxophone, violin, brass bass, traps, conducted by Leonard Joy.   46th St, New York, N.Y., February 21, 1929

48384-1,2	Desert Blues	Vi unissued
48384-3	**Desert Blues** *(Rodgers)*	Vi V-40096, MW M-4451, Zo 5495, RZ T5495, HMV N4351, Vi 21-0176, 27-0102, P282; WPT22, EPAT22, LPT3037, LPM2213, RD27241, DPS2021, RA5460

Vocal and yodelling with own guitar and orchestra: unknown cornet, clarinet, violin, piano, brass bass, conducted by Leonard Joy.

48385-1	**Any Old Time** *(Rodgers)*	Vi 22488, Bb B-5664, MW M-4730, Zo EE221, 5780, RZ T5780, HMV N4215; LPM1640, LSP3315, RD27110, DPS2021, VPS6091, RA5460, RA5510, RA5176, RA9037, DPL2-0075
48385-2	Any Old Time	Vi unissued

Vocal and yodelling with own guitar.   New York, N.Y., February 23, 1929

49990-1	Blue Yodel No. 5	Vi unissued
49990-2	**Blue Yodel No. 5** *(Rodgers)*	Vi 22072, MW M-4212, Zo EE185, 5548, RZ T5548, IZ326, Tw FT1824; LPM1640, RD27110, DPS2021, RA5460
49991-1	High Powered Mama	Vi unissued
49991-2	**High Powered Mama** *(Rodgers)*[7]	Vi 22523, Zo 5808, RZ T5808, IZ334; LPM1640, RD27110, DPS2021, RA5461
49991-3	High Powered Mama	Vi unissued
49992-1	**I'm Sorry We Met** *(Rodgers)*	Vi 22072, Zo EE185, 5548, RZ T5548, IZ326, Tw FT1824, Vi A1466, 21-0177, 27-0103, P282; WPT22, LPT3037, LPM2213, RD27241, DPS2021, RA5461
49992-2	I'm Sorry We Met	Vi unissued

Vocal and yodelling with Joe Kaipo (steel guitar), Billy Burke (guitar), Weldon Burke (ukulele).[8]   Banquet Hall, Jefferson Hotel, Dallas, Tex., August 8, 1929

55307-1	Everybody Does It in Hawaii	Vi unissued
55307-2	**Everybody Does It In Hawaii** *(McWilliams-Rodgers)*	Vi 22143, Zo EE189, 5577, RZ T5577, IZ327, HMV N4364; LPM2634, RD7562, RA5461, DPL2-0075

Bob McGimsey (whistling) added.

55308-1	**Tuck Away My Lonesome Blues** *(Rodgers-Kaipo-McWilliams)*	Vi 22220, Bb B-5664, MW M-5036, Zo EE269, 5983, RZ T5983, Tw FT1356, Vi 21-0181, 27-0105, P318; WPT23, EPAT23, LPT3038, LPM2213, RD27241, DPS2021, RA5461
55308-2,3	Tuck Away My Lonesome Blues	Vi unissued

Vocal, yodelling and train-whistle effects with accompaniment as on 55307.

55309-1	Train Whistle Blues	Vi unissued
55309-2	**Train Whistle Blues** *(Rodgers)*	Vi 22379, MW M-4223, Zo 5697, RZ T5697, G23113, HMV N4345; (A)EP20176, LPM1640, RD27110, DPS2021, RA5461, RA9037

Vocal and yodelling with Joe Kaipo (steel guitar), Billy Burke (guitar).
                                    Same location, August 10, 1929

| 55332-1 | Jimmie's Texas Blues | Vi unissued |
| 55332-2 | **Jimmie's Texas Blues** *(Rodgers)* | Vi 22379, MW M-4212, Zo 5697, RZ T5697, G23113, HMV N4345; LPM1640, RD27110, DPS2021, RA5461, RA9037 |

Vocal and yodelling with own guitar.

| 55333-1 | Frankie and Johnnie | Vi unissued |
| 55333-2 | **Frankie and Johnnie** *(−)*[9] | Vi 22143, Bb B-5223, El 2109, Su S-3306, MW M-4309, M-4721, Zo EE189, 5577, RZ T5577, IZ327, HMV N4371, Vi 21-0044, 27-0100, P244; WPT21, EPAT21, LPT3037, HMV 7EG8163, LPM2213, DPS2021, VPS6091, RA5461, RA5501, RA9037, DPL2-0075 |

Vocal with unknown cornet, saxophone, piano, banjo, string bass.
                                    Same location, August 12, 1929

| 55344-1,2,3 | Frankie and Johnny | Vi unissued |

Vocal and yodelling with own guitar, Joe Kaipo (steel guitar), L. D. Dyke (musical saw).

| 55345-1 | Home Call | Vi unissued |
| 55345-2 | **Home Call** *(Rodgers-McWilliams)* | Vi LPT3073, LPM2213, RD27241, DPS2021, RA5461 |

Dyke absent.

| 55345-3 | Home Call | Vi unissued |

Vocal and yodelling with Joe Kaipo (steel guitar), Billy Burke (guitar), Weldon Burke (ukulele).
                                    Dallas, Tex., October 22, 1929

56449-1,2	Whisper Your Mother's Name	Vi unissued
56449-3	**Whisper Your Mother's Name** *(J. Rodgers-H. Braistead)*	Vi 22319, Bb B-5097, El 1983, Su S-3142, MW M-4207, RZ G23193, MR2242, IZ496, HMV EA 1382, N4310, Tw FT9115; LSP4073, RA5461, DPM2047
56449-4	Whisper Your Mother's Name	Vi unissued

(session continued over)

Vocal and yodelling with own guitar.

56450-1	**The Land of My Boyhood Dreams** *(Rodgers)*	Vi 23811, Bb B-5337, Su S-3418, MW M-4450, M-4728, RZ G23190, HMV EA1303, N4259
56450-2,3	The Land of My Boyhood Dreams	Vi unissued
56450-4	**The Land of My Boyhood Dreams**	Vi LPM2865, RD7644, RA5461
56453-1,2	Blue Yodel No. 6	Vi unissued
56453-3	**Blue Yodel No. 6** *(Rodgers)*	Vi 22271, MW M-4211, Zo 5623, RZ T5623, IZ329, Vi 21-0182, 27-0106, P318; WPT23, EPAT410, LPT3039, LPM1232, RD27138, RA5461, DPM2047
56454-1,2	Yodelling Cowboy	Vi unissued
56454-3	**Yodelling Cowboy** *(Rodgers-McWilliams)*	Vi 22271, Bb B-5991, MW M-4058, M-4213, Zo 5623, RZ T5623, IZ 329, HMV N4381; LPM2531, LSP4073, RD7505, RA5461

Joe Kaipo (steel guitar) added.

56455-1	**My Rough and Rowdy Ways** *(Rodgers-McWilliams)*	Vi 22220, MW M-4215, Zo EE269, 6022, RZ T6022, Tw FT1808; LPM2112, RD27203, L10883, VPS6091, RA5461, DPL2-0075
56455-2,3	My Rough and Rowdy Ways	Vi unissued

Kaipo absent.

56456-1	**I've Ranged, I've Roamed and I've Travelled**	Vi LPM2865, RD7644, RA5461, DPL2-0075
56456-2	I've Ranged, I've Roamed and I've Travelled	Vi unissued
56456-3	**I've Ranged, I've Roamed and I've Travelled** *(Rodgers-McWilliams)*	Bb B-5892, MW M-5013, RZ G23205, HMV EA1566, N4377

Note: *the take details of 56456 have not been verified. Masters 56451-2 were by the Burke Brothers.*

Vocal, yodelling and train-whistle effects, with Billy Burke (guitar).
New Orleans, La., November 13, 1929

56528-1	**Hobo Bill's Last Ride** *(Waldo Lafayette O'Neal)*	Vi 22421, MW M-4210, Zo EE213, 5724, RZ T5724, IZ333, Tw FT1784; (A)EP20176, LPM1640, RD27110, DPS2021, RA5461, RA5510, RA5176, RA9037
56528-2,3	Hobo Bill's Last Ride	Vi unissued

Vocal and yodelling with Billy Burke (guitar).

Atlanta, Ga., November 25, 1929

56594-1,2	Mississippi River Blues	Vi unissued
56594-3	**Mississippi River Blues** *(Rodgers)*	Vi 23535, Bb B-5393, MW M-4722, Zo 5983, RZ T5983, G23199, HMV EA1402, N4207, Tw FT1356; LPM2531, RD7505, RA5462, RA9038, DPM2047
56595-1,2,3	Nobody Knows But Me	Vi unissued
56595-4	**Nobody Knows But Me** *(McWilliams-Rodgers)*	Vi 23518, MW M-4724, RZ G23198, HMV EA1401, N4322, Tw FT9116; LPM2634, RD7562, RA5462

Vocal and yodelling with own guitar, Billy Burke (guitar).

Same location, November 26, 1929

| 56607-1 | **Anniversary Blue Yodel (Blue Yodel No. 7)** *(Rodgers-McWilliams)* | Vi 22488, MW M-4210, Zo EE221, 5780, RZ T5780, HMV N4215; LPT3073, LPM2213, RD27242, DPS2021, RA5462 |
| 56607-2,3 | Anniversary Blue Yodel | Vi unissued |

Burke absent.

| 56608-1 | **She Was Happy Till She Met You** *(Rodgers-McWilliams)* | Vi 23681, Bb B-5057, El 1983, Su S-3142, MW M-4207, M-4324, Zo EE352, RZ MR1335, IZ388, Tw FT1723; LPM2531, RD7505, RA5462 |

Vocal and yodelling with Billy Burke (guitar).

| 56608-2,3 | She Was Happy Till She Met You | Vi unissued |

Vocal and yodelling with own guitar, Billy Burke (guitar).

Same location, November 27, 1929

| 56617-1 | **Blue Yodel No. 11** *(Rodgers)* | Vi 23796, MW M-4726; LPM2634, RD7562, RA5462, DPM2047 |
| 56617-2,3,4 | Blue Yodel No. 11 | Vi unissued |

Vocal and yodelling with Billy Burke (guitar)

Same location, November 28, 1929

56618-1	**A Drunkard's Child** *(Jenkins-Rodgers)*	Vi 22319, MW M-4221, Zo 4343, RZ G23194, HMV EA1385; LPM2634, RD7562, RA5462, DPM2047
56618-2,3	A Drunkard's Child	Vi unissued
56619-1	**That's Why I'm Blue** *Blue (Mc Williams-Rodgers)*	Vi 22421, Bb B-6198, MW M-4222, Zo EE213, 5724, RZ T5724, MR2049, IZ333, IZ422, Tw FT1784; LPM2865, RD7644, RA5462
56619-2,3	That Why I'm Blue	Vi unissued
56620-1,2,3	Why Did You Give Me Your Love?	Vi unissued
56620-4	**Why Did You Give Me Your Love?** *(Rodgers)*	Bb B-5892, MW M-5013, RZ G23205, HMV EA1566, N4377; LPM2865, LSP3315, RD7644, RA5462, DPM2047

Vocal with Bob Sawyer's Jazz Band: Mickey Bloom (cornet), Boyd Senter (clarinet), Bob Sawyer (piano), unknown banjo.

Hollywood Recording Studios, Los Angeles, Ca., June 30, 1930

54849-1	My Blue-Eyed Jane	Vi unissued
54849-2	**My Blue-Eyed Jane** *(Lulu Belle White-Jimmie Rodgers)*	Vi 23549, Bb B-5393, MW M-4222, RZ G23196, HMV EA1399, N4302, Tw FT9114; LPM2112, RD27203, L10883, RA5462, DPL2-0075
54849-3	My Blue-Eyed Jane	Vi unissued

Vocal (and yodelling*) with Lani McIntyre's Hawaiians: unknown steel guitar, guitar, ukulele, string bass.

54850-1,2	*Why Should I Be Lonely?	Vi unissued
54850-3	*Why Should I Be Lonely? *(Estelle Lovell-Jimmie Rodgers)*	Vi 23609, Bb B-5082, Su S-3169, MW M-4204, Zo EE305, 6102, RZ T6102, IZ336, HMV N4221; LPM2634, LSP3315, RD7562, RA5462, RA9038
54851-1,2	Moonlight and Skies	Vi unissued
54851-3	**Moonlight and Skies** *(Raymond Hall-Jimmie Rodgers)*	Vi 23574, Bb B-5000, El 1830, 1958, Su S-3104, MW M-4216, M-4720, Zo EE369, RZ MR2200, IZ469, HMV MH187, N4322, Tw FT9116, Co IFB341; LPM2634, LSP3315, RD7562, RA5462, RA5510, DPL2-0075

Vocal and yodelling with own guitar.   Same location, July 1, 1930

54852-1	Pistol Packin' Papa	Vi unissued
54852-2	**Pistol Packin' Papa** *(Rodgers-O'Neal)*	Vi 22554, MW M-4316, M-4730, Zo EE232, 4342, 6011, RZ T6011, Vi 420-0027, 447-0027; EPAT410, PT3035, LPT3039, LPM1232, RD27138, VPS6091, RA5462, DPM2047

Vocal and yodelling with Lani McIntyre's Hawaiians (as on 54850).
                                                         Same location, July 2, 1930

54854-1,2	Take Me Back Again	Vi unissued
54854-3	**Take Me Back Again** *(Hill-Rodgers)*	Bb B-7600, HMV N4422; LPM2634, RD7562, RA5462

Note: *the take details of 54854 cannot be verified.*

Vocal and yodelling with Lani McIntyre (guitar).   Same location, July 5, 1930

54855-1	**Those Gambler's Blues** $(-)^{10}$	Vi 22554, MW M-4211, Zo EE232, 4344, RZ MR911; LPM2865, RD7644, RA5463
54855-2,3	Those Gambler's Blues	Vi unissued

Vocal (and yodelling*) with Lani McIntyre's Hawaiians (as on 54850).
                                                         Same location, July 7, 1930

54856-1	I'm Lonesome Too	Vi unissued
54856-2	**I'm Lonesome Too** *(Rodgers)*	Vi 23564, Bb B-5739, MW M-4220, RZ G23189, MR1599, IZ401, HMV EA1253, Tw FT1822; LPM2531, RD7505, RA5463
54856-3	I'm Lonesome Too	Vi unissued
54857-1,2	*The One Rose (That's Left in My Heart)	Vi unissued
54857-3	***The One Rose (That's Left In My Heart)** *(Mel Lyon-Lani McIntyre)*	Bb B-7280; LPM2112, RD27203, L10883, RA5463, RA5510, RA5176, RA9038

Note: *the take details of 54857 cannot be verified.*

Vocal and yodelling with Lani McIntyre's Hawaiians: unknown steel guitar, piano, , guitar, string bass.   Same location, July 8, 1930

54860-1,2	For the Sake of Days Gone By	Vi unissued

                                                         Same location, July 9, 1930

54860-3	**For the Sake of Days Gone By** *(Rodgers-White)*	Vi 23651, Bb B-5784, MW M-4221, Zo EE363, HMV N4281, Vi A1430; LPM2531, RD7505, RA5463, DPM2047
54860-4	For the Sake of Days Gone By	Vi unissued

Vocal and yodelling with Bob Sawyer's Jazz Band: as on 54849, with unknown brass bass added.　　　　　　　　　　　　　　　Same location, July 10, 1930

54861-1,2	Jimmie's Mean Mama Blues	Vi unissued
54861-3	**Jimmie's Mean Mama Blues**	Vi 23503, MW M-4723,
	(O'Neal-Sawyer)	Zo 5859, RZ T5859, G23115,
		HMV EA1541, Vi 420-0027,
		447-0027; EPAT410, PT3035,
		LPT3039, LPM1232, RD27138,
		RA5463

Vocal and yodelling (and train-whistle effects†) with own guitar.
　　　　　　　　　　　　　　　　　　　　　Same location, July 11, 1930

54862-1,2	†The Mystery of Number Five	Vi unissued
54862-3	**†The Mystery of Number Five**	Vi 23518, Bb B-5739,
	(Rodgers)	MW M-4223, Zo 4343,
		RZ G23198, MR1599, IZ401,
		HMV EA1401, Tw FT1822;
		LPM2865, LSP3315, RD7644,
		RA5463, DPM2047
54863-1	**Blue Yodel No. 8** (Mule	Vi 23503, Bb B-6275,
	Skinner Blues) *(Rodgers)*	MW M-4723, M-8235, Zo 5859,
		RZ T5859, G23115,
		HMV EA1541; LPT3073,
		LPM2112, LSP3315, L10883,
		RD27203, VPS6091, RA5463,
		RA5510, RA5176, RA9038
54863-2,3	Blue Yodel No. 8	Vi unissued

　　　　　　　　　　　　　　　　　　　　　Same location, July 12, 1930

54864-1	**In the Jailhouse Now, No. 2**	Vi 22523, MW M-4315,
	(Rodgers)[11]	Zo 5808, RZ T5808, IZ334;
		LPT3073, LPM2112, RD27203,
		L10883, RA5463, RA5501
54864-2,3	In the Jailhouse Now, No. 2	Vi unissued

Vocal and yodelling with Louis Armstrong (cornet), Lil Armstrong (piano).[12]
　　　　　　　　　　　　　　　　　　　　　Same location, July 16, 1930

54867-1	Blue Yodel No. 9	Vi unissued
54867-2	**Blue Yodel No. 9** *(Rodgers)*	Vi 23580, MW M-4209,
		M-4724, Zo EE300, RZ MR3208,
		HMV MH194, Tw FT8832,
		Co MZ315; LPM2112, RD27203,
		L10883, RA5463, RA5510,
		RA5176
54867-3	Blue Yodel No. 9	Vi unissued

Dialogue with I. N. Bronsen.　　　　　　　　Same location, July 17, 1930

| 1302 | The Pullman Porters | Vi unissued |

Vocal and yodelling with own guitar, Charles Kama (steel guitar).

Texas Hotel, San Antonio, Tex., January 31, 1931

67133-1,2	T. B. Blues	Vi unissued
67133-3	**T. B. Blues** *(Rodgers-Hall)*	Vi 23535, Bb B-6275, MW M-4067, M-4729, Zo 4344, RZ G23199, MR911, MR2374, IZ616, HMV EA1402; LPM2531, RD7505, RA5463

Shelly Lee Alley, Alvin Alley (fiddles), M. T. Salazar (guitar) and Mike Cordova (string bass) added.

67134-1	Travellin' Blues	Vi unissued
67134-2	**Travellin' Blues** *(Jimmie Rodgers-Shelly Lee Alley)*	Vi 23564, MW M-4729, RZ G23112, HMV EA1514, N4367; LPT3073, LPM2112, RD27203, L10883, RA5463, DPM2047
67134-3	Travellin' Blues	Vi unissued

Shelly Lee Alley and Alvin Alley absent.

67135-1	**Jimmie the Kid** *(Rodgers-Neville)*	Vi 23549, MW M-4731, Zo 6022, RZ T6022, G23196, MR3208, HMV EA1399, N4302, MH194, Tw FT8832, FT9114; LPM2213, DPS2021, RD27241, RA5463, RA5501, DPL2-0075
67135-2,3	Jimmie the Kid	Vi unissued

Vocal and yodelling with own guitar, Sara Carter (vocal, yodelling, guitar).

Louisville, Ky., June 10, 1931

69412-1	**Why There's a Tear in My Eye** *(A. P. Carter)*	Bb B-6698, MW M-7138, RZ MR2374, MR2429, ME33, IZ616, IZ649, Tw FT8313
69412-2	Why There's a Tear in My Eye	Vi unissued
69412-3	**Why There's a Tear in My Eye**	Vi LPM2865, RD7644, RA5463, RA5501, DPM2047
69413-1	The Wonderful City	Vi unissued
69413-2	**The Wonderful City** *(Rodgers-McWilliams)*	Bb B-6810, MW M-7137, RZ G23184, MR2455, IZ662, Tw FT8313; LPM2865, RD7644, RA5464, RA5501, DPM2047
69413-3	The Wonderful City	Vi unissued

Vocal and yodelling with Clifford Gibson (guitar)

Same location, June 11, 1931

| 69424-1,2 | Let Me Be Your Sidetrack | Vi unissued |

Vocal and yodelling with own guitar.

69424-3	**Let Me Be Your Sidetrack**	Vi 23621, Bb B-5084, Su S-3171,
	(Rodgers)	MW M-4209, Zo EE363, 6056,
		RZ T6056, HMV N4209;
		LPM1640, RD27110, DPS2021,
		RA5464
69424-4	Let Me Be Your Sidetrack	Vi unissued

Vocal, speech and yodelling with A. P. Carter (vocal, speech), Sara Carter (vocal, speech, guitar), Maybelle Carter (vocal, speech, mandolin).

| 69427-1,2 | Jimmie Rodgers Visits the Carter Family | Vi unissued |
| 69427-3 | **Jimmie Rodgers Visits the Carter Family** | Vi RA5645 |

Vocal, speech, yodelling and guitar, with A. P. Carter (speech), Sara Carter (vocal speech, yodelling), Maybelle Carter (speech).

| 69428-1,2 | The Carter Family Visits Jimmie Rodgers[13] | Vi unissued |
| 69428-3 | **The Carter Family Visits Jimmie Rodgers** | Vi RA5645[14] |

Vocal, speech and yodelling with A. P. Carter (vocal, speech), Sara Carter (vocal, speech, guitar), Maybelle Carter (vocal, speech, mandolin).

Same location, June 12, 1931

69427-4	**Jimmie Rodgers Visits the Carter Family**	Vi 23574, MW M-4720,
		Zo EE369, RZ MR3164, ME34,
		HMV MH188, Tw FT8806;
		LPM2865, RD7644, RA5464,
		RA5501, RA5645[15]

Note: *the above recording contains* My Clinch Mountain Home *(vocal duet by Sara and Maybelle with own guitar and mandolin);* Little Darling Pal of Mine *(vocal duet by Sara and Maybelle with guitar); and* Hot Time in the Old Town Tonight *(vocal quartet with yodelling by Rodgers and guitar by Sara).*

Vocal, speech, yodelling and guitar with A. P. Carter (speech), Sara Carter (vocal, speech, yodelling), Maybelle Carter (speech).

69428-4	**The Carter Family and Jimmie Rodgers in Texas**	Bb B-6762, MW M-7137,
		RZ MR3164, ME34, HMV MH188,
		Tw FT8806; LPM2865, RD7644,
		RA5464, RA5501, RA5645,
		DPL2-0075

Note: *the above recording contains* Yodelling Cowboy *(vocal, yodelling and guitar by Rodgers) and* T for Texas *(vocal and yodelling by Rodgers and Sara Carter with guitar by Rodgers).*

Vocal and yodelling with Cliff Carlisle (steel guitar), Wilbur Ball (guitar).

Same location, June 13, 1931

69432-1	When the Cactus Is in Bloom	Vi unissued
69432-2	**When the Cactus Is in Bloom**	Vi 23636, Bb B-5163, El 2060,
	(Rodgers)	Su S-3244, MW M-4216,
		Zo EE345, RZ MR2795,[16]
		Tw FT8585; LPM2531, RD7505,
		RA5464, RA9038, DPM2047
69432-3	When the Cactus Is in Bloom	Vi unissued

Vocal and yodelling with Ruth Ann Moore (piano).

Same location, June 15, 1931

69439-1	Gambling Polka Dot Blues	Vi unissued
69439-2	**Gambling Polka Dot Blues**	Vi 23636, Zo 4365, EE345;
	(Rodgers-Hall)	LPM2865, RD7644, RA5464
69439-3	Gambling Polka Dot Blues	Vi unissued

Vocal and yodelling with own ukulele, Cliff Carlisle (steel guitar), Wilbur Ball (guitar).

69443-1,2	Looking For a New Mama	Vi unissued
69443-3	**Looking For a New Mama**	Vi 23580, Bb B-5037, El 1966,
	(Rodgers)	Su S-3131, MW M-4203,
		Zo EE300, RZ MR3002,
		MR20215, ME15, Tw FT8694;
		LPM2213, RD27241, DPS2021,
		RA5464

Vocal and yodelling with Ruth Ann Moore (piano).

Same location, June 16, 1931

| 69448-1 | **What's It?** (My Dog-Faced Gal) *(Rodgers-Neville)*[17] | Vi 23609, Bb B-5084, Su S-3171, MW M-4208, Zo EE305; LPM2865, RD7644, RA5464 |
| 69448-2,3,4 | What's It? | Vi unissued |

Vocal and yodelling with the Louisville Jug Band: George Allen (clarinet), Clifford Hayes (fiddle), Cal Smith, Freddie Smith (guitars), Earl McDonald (jug).

69449-1,2	My Good Gal's Gone—Blues	Vi unissued
69449-3	**My Good Gal's Gone—Blues**	Bb B-5942, MW M-5014,
	(Rodgers)	Tw FT1925;[18] LPM1640,
		RD27110, DPS2021, RA5464

Vocal, yodelling and train-whistle effect with own guitar.

Same location, June 17, 1931

69458-1	**Southern Cannon-Ball**	Vi 23811, MW M-4728,
	(J. Rodgers-R. Hall)	RZ G23111, HMV EA1503,
		N4259; LPM2112, RD27203,
		L10883, RA5464, RA5501,
		DPM2047
69458-2,3,4	Southern Cannon-Ball	Vi unissued

Dubbing session.   Camden, N. J., October 27, 1931

69032-1,2   Jimmie Rodgers' Puzzle Record Vi unissued

Same location, November 11, 1931

69032-3   **Jimmie Rodgers' Puzzle Record**
             Train Whistle Blues
             Blue Yodel
             Everybody Does It in   Vi 23621, Zo 4365, 6056,
               Hawaii   RZ T6056, G23204,
                                      HMV EA1489, N4209
69032-4   Jimmie Rodgers' Puzzle Record Vi unissued

Note: *Rodgers was not present at either of these sessions. The three tracks listed were dubbed, in edited forms, on to a novelty record with three concentric grooves, starting at different points on the record's circumference. Though Victor files show the title as above, all issues are labelled* Rodgers Puzzle Record.

Vocal and yodelling with Dick Bunyard (steel guitar), Bill Boyd (guitar), Red Young (mandolin), Fred Koons (string bass).
                     Ball Room, Jefferson Hotel, Dallas, Tex., February 2, 1932

70645-1   Roll Along, Kentucky Moon   Vi unissued
70645-2   **Roll Along, Kentucky Moon**   Vi 23651, Bb B-5082, Su S-3169,
              (Bill Halley)   MW M-4219, Zo 4370,
                                      RZ G23188, MR3122, IZ1004,
                                      HMV EA1228, N4281,
                                      Tw FT8775, Vi A1430; LPM2531,
                                      LSP3315, RD7505, RA5464,
                                      RA5501, RA9038, DPM2047,
                                      DPL2-0075

Train-whistle effects and guitar also by Rodgers.   Same location, February 3, 1932

70646-1   **Hobo's Meditation** *(Rodgers)*   Vi 23711, MW M-4205, Zo 4374,
                                      RZ G23192, MR3313, MR20064,
                                      IZ1065, HMV EA1374, N4233,
                                      Tw FT8902; LPM2634, RD7562,
                                      RA5464, RA9038
70646-2   Hobo's Meditation   Vi unissued

Vocal and yodelling with Billy Burke (steel guitar), Weldon Burke (guitar), Charlie Burke (ukulele), Fred Koons (string bass).   Same location, February 4, 1932

70647-1,2   My Time Ain't Long   Vi unissued
70647-3   **My Time Ain't Long** *(Rodgers-*   Vi 23669, Bb B-5083, El 2009,
              O'Neal)   Su S-3170, Zo 6159, RZ T6159,
                                      HMV N4210; LPM2865, RD7644,
                                      RA5464, DPM2047

Billy Burke plays standard guitar; Charlie Burke absent.

70648-1   Ninety-Nine Years Blues   Vi unissued
70648-2   **Ninety-Nine Years Blues**   Vi 23669, MW M-4215, Zo 6159,
             (Rodgers-Hall)   RZ T6159, HMV N4210;
                                      LPM2634, RD7562, RA5464

45091-4	Mississippi Moon	Vi unissued
45091-5	**Mississippi Moon** *(Rodgers-McWilliams)*	Vi 23696, Bb B-5136, El 2042, Su S-3217, MW M-4220, RZ G23189, MR1853, IZ410, HMV EA1253, N4292, Vi A1401, JA708; LPM2112, RD27203, L10883, RA5465, RA5510, RA5176, DPM2047

Vocal and yodelling with own guitar, Fred Coon[19] (guitar).

Same location, February 5, 1932

45091-3	Mississippi Moon	Vi unissued
70649-1	**Down the Old Road to Home** *(J. Rodgers-Carey D. Harvey)*	Vi 23711, Bb B-5081, Su S-3168, MW M-4202, RZ G23192, MR1725, IZ404, HMV EA1374; LPM1640, RD27110, RA5465, RA9038, DPS2021
70649-2	Down the Old Road to Home	Vi unissued

Coon absent.

Same location, February 6, 1932

70650-1	**Blue Yodel No. 10** *(Rodgers)*	Vi 23696, MW M-4203, M-4725, RZ MR3257, MR20010, HMV N4292, Tw FT8858, Vi A1401,[20] JA708,[20] Co MZ315; LPM2634, RD7562, RA5465
70650-2	Blue Yodel No. 10	Vi unissued
55345-4	**Home Call** *(Rodgers-McWilliams)*	Vi 23681, MW M-4219, Zo EE352, HMV N4367

Vocal and yodelling with Clayton McMichen (fiddle), Slim Bryant (guitar), Oddie McWindows (banjo), George Howell (string bass).

Church Studio No. 2, Camden, N. J., August 10, 1932

58960-1,2,3,3A,4,4A,5,5A,[21]

In the Hills of Tennessee	Vi unissued

Note: *take 3A was experimentally processed but no extant copy has been traced.*

Howell absent.

Same location, August 11, 1932

58961-1,1A,2	Mother, the Queen of My Heart	Vi unissued
58961-2A	**Mother, the Queen of My Heart** *(Hoyt Bryant-J. Rodgers)*	Vi 23721, Bb B-5080, El 2008, Su S-3167, MW M-4206, RZ G23195, MR1310, HMV EA1390, N4239; LPT3073, LPM2213, LSP3315, RD27241, RA5465, RA5510, RA5176, RA9038, DPL2-0075
58962-1,1A	Prohibition Has Done Me Wrong	Vi unissued[22]

(session continued over)

58963-1	Rock All Our Babies to Sleep	Vi unissued
58963-1A	**Rock All Our Babies to Sleep** *(—)*	Vi 23721, Bb B-5000; El 1830, 1958, Su S-3104, MW M-4201, Zo 4378, RZ G23200, MR2200, IZ469, HMV EA1403, N4239, MH187, Co IFB341; LPM2634, RD7562, RA5465, DPM2047
58964-1,1A	Whippin' That Old T.B.	Vi unissued
58964-2	**Whippin' That Old T.B.** *(Rodgers)*	Vi 23751, Bb B-5076, El 1999, Su S-3157, MW M-4204, RZ G23195, MR1310, HMV EA1390; LPM2634, RD7562, RA5465
58964-2A	Whippin' That Old T.B.	Vi unissued

Vocal and yodelling with own guitar, Slim Bryant (guitar).

Same location, August 15, 1932

58968-1,1A,2	No Hard Times	Vi unissued
58968	**No Hard Times** *(Rodgers)*	Vi 23751, MW M-4205, RZ G23117, HMV N4251; LPM1640, RD27110, DPS2021, RA5465
58968-3,3A	No Hard Times	Vi unissued

Oddie McWindows (banjo) replaces Bryant.

58969-1	Long Tall Mama Blues	Vi unissued
58969-1A	**Long Tall Mama Blues** *(Rodgers)*	Vi 23766, MW M-4202, HMV N4245; LPM2112, RD27203, L10883, RA5465

As on 58961-64

58970-1,1A,2	Peach-Pickin' Time Down in Georgia	Vi unissued
58970-2A	**Peach-Pickin' Time Down in Georgia** *(Rodgers-McMichen)*	Vi 23781, Bb B-5080, El 2008, Su S-3167, MW M-4200, RZ G23200, MR1335, IZ388, HMV EA1403, N4242, Tw FT1723; LPT3073, LPM2112, RD27203, L10883, RA5465, VPS6091, RA5501, SRA5040, RA5524, RA9038, DPL2-0075
58971-1,2	Gambling Barroom Blues	Vi unissued
58971-3	**Gambling Barroom Blues** *(Jimmie Rodgers-Shelly Lee Alley)*	Vi 23766, Bb B-5037, El 1966, Su S-3131, MW M-4203, RZ G23112, ME15, MR3002, MR20215, HMV EA1514, N4245, Tw FT8694; LPM2531, RD7505, RA5465, DPM2047
58972-1	**I've Only Loved Three Women** *(Jimmie Rodgers-Carey D. Harvey)*	Bb B-6810, MW M-7138, RZ G23184, MR2455, IZ662, Tw FT8334; LPM2865, RD7644, RA5465

Vocal and yodelling with unknown clarinet, two violins, piano, guitar.
Studio No.1, East 24th St, New York, N.Y., August 29, 1932

73324-1	**In the Hills of Tennessee** *(Sam Lewis-Ira Schuster)*	Vi 23736, Bb B-5784, MW M-4200, Zo 4376, RZ G23201, MR2700, HMV EA1404, N4234, Tw FT8538; LPM2865, RD7644, RA5465
73325-1	**Prairie Lullaby** *(George Brown-Jimmie Rodgers)* [2] [3]	Vi 23781, Bb B-5076, El 1999, Su S-3157, MW M-4201, RZ G23203, MR1725, IZ404, HMV EA1405, N4242, Vi 420-0028, 447-0028; EPAT411, PT3035, LPT3039, LPT3073, (A)EP21002, LPM1232, RD27138, RA5465
73326-1	**Miss the Mississippi and You** *(Bill Halley)*	Vi 23736, Bb B-5081, Su S-3168, MW M-4206, Zo 4376, RZ G23201, MR3257, MR20010, HMV EA1404, N4234, Tw FT8858; LPM2213, RD27241, RA5466, RA9038, DPS2021
73327-1	**Sweet Mama Hurry Home** **(or I'll Be Gone)** *(Jack Neville)*	Vi 23796, MW M-4726, RZ G23202, HMV EA1406; LPM2531, RD7505, RA5466

Vocal and yodelling with own guitar.   Same location, May 17, 1933

76138-1	**Blue Yodel No. 12** (Barefoot Blues *(J. Rodgers)*	Vi 24456, 18-6000, MW M-4727; LPM2213, RD27241, DPS2021, RA5466
76139-1	**Dreaming With Tears in My** **Eyes** *(O'Neal-Rodgers)*	Vi LPM2531, RD7505, RA5466
76140-1	**The Cowhand's Last Ride** *(Jimmie Rodgers-Arza Hitt)*	Vi 24456, 18-6000, MW M-4727, RZ G23191, HMV EA1362; LPM2531, RD7505, RA5466
76141-1	**I'm Free (From the Chain** **Gang Now)** *(Lou Herscher)*	Vi 23830, MW M-4453, RZ G23204, HMV EA1489, N4263, Tw FT9112; LPM2531, RD7505, RA5466

Same location, May 18, 1933

76139-2	**Dreaming With Tears in My** **Eyes**	Bb B-7600, MW M-7139, HMV N4422
76151-1	**Yodelling My Way Back Home** *(Jimmie Rodgers)*	Bb B-7280, MW M-7139, RZ MR2700, Tw FT8538; LPM2634, RD7562, RA5466
76160-1	**Jimmie Rodgers Last Blue** **Yodel** *(Jimmie Rodgers)*	Bb B-5281, El 2155, Su S-3362, MW M-4415, RZ G23206, MR1702, HMV EA1567, Tw FT1874; LPM2112, RD27203, L10883, RA5466, RA9038, DPM2047, DPL2-0075

Same location, May 20, 1933

76191-1   **The Yodelling Ranger**   Vi 23830, Bb B-5556,
            (Jimmie Rodgers-Raymond   MW M-4453, RZ G23203,
            Hall)   MR1853, IZ410, HMV EA1405,
                                    N4263, Tw FT9112; RA5466,
                                    DPM2047, CMH CMH106

76192-1   **Old Pal of My Heart**   Vi 23816, Bb B-5136, El 2042,
            (John B. Mason-Jimmie   Su S-3217, RZ G23191,
            Rodgers)   Zo 4378, RZ MR2242, IZ496,
                                    HMV EA1362, Tw FT8185,
                                    Vi 420-0029, 447-0029;
                                    EPAT411, PT3035, LPT3039,
                                    LPM1232, RD27138, RA5466,
                                    DPM2047

Vocal and yodelling with Tony Colicchio (steel guitar), John Cali (guitar).[24]

Same location, May 24, 1933

76327-1   **Old Love Letters (Bring**   Vi 23840, Bb B-6198,
            Memories of You)   MW M-4454, RZ G23190,
            (Rodgers-Herscher-Butcher)   MR2049, IZ422, HMV EA1303,
                                    N4297, Tw FT9113; LPM2531,
                                    RD7505, RA5466

Colicchio plays standard guitar and Cali banjo.

76328-1   **Mississippi Delta Blues**   Vi 23816, RZ G23194,
            (Neville-Rodgers)   HMV EA1385; LPM1640,
                                    RD27110, DPS2021, RA5466

Colicchio and Cali both play standard guitars.

76331-1   **Somewhere Down Below the**   Vi 23840, MW M-4454,
            Dixon Line *(Ryan-Rodgers)*   RZ G23111, HMV EA1503,
                                    N4297, Tw FT9113;
                                    (A)EP20176, LPM1640,
                                    RD27110, DPS2021, RA5176,
                                    RA5466, RA5510

Vocal and yodelling with own guitar.

76332,-1   **Fifteen Years Ago Today**[25]   Bb B-5281, El 2155,
            (Herscher-Richards-   Su S-3362, MW M-4415,
            Rodgers)   RZ G23206, MR1702, MR3313,
                                    MR20064, IZ1065,
                                    HMV EA1567, Tw FT1874,
                                    FT8902; LPM2634, RD7562,
                                    RA5466

Dubbing session.

Columbia Graphophone Co. studios, London, England, October 28, 1935

WAR3690-1	**Jimmie Rodgers Medley, Part 1** Intro: My Old Pal: Dear Old Sunny South; Blue Yodel No. 1	RZ MR1918, G22792, 1Z414, Tw FT1980
WAR3690-2	Jimmie Rodgers Medley, Part 1	Co rejected
WAR3691-1	**Jimmie Rodgers Medley, Part 2** Intro.: Daddy and Home; Away Out on the Mountain; Blue Yodel No. 4	RZ MR1918, G22792, 1Z414, Tw FT1980
WAR3691-2	Jimmie Rodgers Medley, Part 2	Co rejected

The following sessions were overdubs by Hank Snow's Rainbow Ranch Boys: Tommy Vaden (fiddle), Joe Talbot (steel guitar), Chet Atkins (guitar, leader), Ernie Newton (string bass).

Victor Studios, Nashville, Tenn., March 18, 1955

F2-WB-0281	**In the Jailhouse Now—No.2**	Vi 20-6092, 47-6092, HMV MH193; LPM2564
F2-WB-0282	**Muleskinner Blues**[26]	Vi 20-6205, 47-6205; LPM2633
F2-WB-0283	**Peach Pickin' Time Down in Georgia**	Vi 20-6092, 47-6092, HMV MH193; CAL737
F2-WB-0284	**Mother, the Queen of My Heart**	Vi 20-6205, 47-6205

Same location, July 22, 1955

F2-WB-3952	**Never No Mo' Blues**	Vi 20-6408, 47-6408
F2-WB-3953	Blue Yodel	Vi unissued
F2-WB-3954	**Daddy and Home**	Vi 20-6408, 47-6408
F2-WB-3955	Memphis Yodel	Vi unissued

Tribute Recordings

GENE AUTRY: vocal and yodelling with Pete Canova (fiddle), Don Weston (guitar).
New York, N.Y., June 22, 1933

| 13494-2 | The Death of Jimmie Rodgers | Ba 32800, Me M12733, Or 8246, Pe 12922, Ro 5246, Vo 5504, Cq 8168, Me 91575, RZ G22176 |
| 13496-1 | The Life of Jimmie Rodgers | Ba 32800, Me M12733, Or 8246, Pe 12922, Ro 5246, Vo 5504, Cq 8168, Me 91575, RZ G22175 |

DWIGHT BUTCHER: vocal and yodelling with own guitar, Prince Wong (fiddle), Lou Herscher (vocal).
New York, N.Y., late June 1933

| C-2099 | When Jimmie Rodgers Said Goodbye | Crown 3516 |

Note: *issued as by* SLIM OAKDALE TRIO.

W. LEE O'DANIEL AND HIS LIGHT CRUST DOUGHBOYS: Clifford Gross (fiddle), Leon McAuliffe (steel guitar) Leon Huff (vocal, guitar), Herman Arnspiger (guitar), C. G. 'Sleepy' Johnson (tenor banjo), Ramon DeArman (string bass), W. Lee O Daniel (leader).

Chicago, Ill., October 11, 1933

| C630-1 | Memories of Jimmy Rodgers | Vo 02605, RZ G22177, Pana 25622 |

GENE AUTRY: vocal and yodelling with Pete Canova (fiddle), Don Weston (guitar).
Chicago, Ill., November 1, 1933

| C 656-1 | When Jimmie Rodgers Said Goodbye | Ba 32902, Me M12843, Or 8283, Pe 12957, Ro 5283, Cq 8246 |
| C-657-1 | Good Luck Old Pal | issues as above |

BRADLEY KINCAID: vocal with own guitar.   New York, N.Y., February 13, 1934

81387-2	Jimmie Rodgers' Life	Bb B-5377, Su S-3458, MW M-4456
81388-1	The Death of Jimmie Rodgers	Bb B-5377, Su S-3458, MW M-4456
81389-1	Mrs. Jimmie Rodgers' Lament	Bb B-5423, MW M-4457, RZ G22367

ASHER SIZEMORE & LITTLE JIMMIE: vocal duet with Asher Sizemore (guitar).
San Antonio, Tex., April 2, 1934

| 82750-1 | Little Jimmie's Goodbye to Jimmie Rodgers | Bb B-5445, RZ G22467, MR2145, IZ514, Tw FT8106 |

Note: *this is a version of* When Jimmie Rodgers Said Goodbye.

BRADLEY KINCAID: vocal with own guitar.   New York, N.Y., May 7, 1934

| 82388-1 | The Death of Jimmie Rodgers | Bb B-5486; LSP4073 |
| 82389-1 | The Life of Jimmie Rodgers | Bb B-5486; LSP4073 |

Note: *these are different songs from those with similar titles recorded by Gene Autry (above).*

KENNETH HOUCHINS: vocal and yodelling with own guitar.
Richmond, Ind., May 1934

| 19595 | When Jimmie Rodgers Said Goodbye | Ch 16781, 45062, MW M-4926 |
| 19596 | Good Luck Old Pal | Ch 16781, 45062, De X1235 |

MRS. JIMMIE RODGERS: vocal with Ernest Tubb (guitar).
San Antonio, Tex., October 26, 1936

| 02935-1 | We Miss Him When The Evening Shadows Fall | Bb B-6698, MW M-7085, RZ MR2429, ME33; LSP4073 |

ERNEST TUBB: vocal and yodelling with own guitar.
Same location, October 27, 1936

| 02952-1 | The Passing of Jimmie Rodgers | Bb B-6693, RZ G23183, Tw FT8228; LSP4073 |
| 02953-1 | The Last Thoughts of Jimmie Rodgers | issues as above |

POSTWAR TRIBUTE RECORDINGS:
A Representative Selection

JIMMIE SKINNER *Jimmie's Yodel Blues* (Radio Artists 255)

YODELING HANK *Jimmie Sings No More Blue Yodels* (Disc)

JIMMY WALKER *Ghost Train* [contains a passing reference to Rodgers] (London 16026)

HANK SNOW & JIMMIE RODGERS SNOW *When Jimmie Rodgers Said Goodbye* (Vi 20-5221; EPB3131, LPM3131, LSP4073)

VIRGINIA ROUNDERS *Hank Williams Meets Jimmie Rodgers* (Rosemay 1)

RILEY CRABTREE *When Hank Williams Meets Jimmie Rodgers* (Columbia 21218)

ERNEST TUBB *When Jimmie Rodgers Said Goodbye/The Last Thoughts of Jimmie Rodgers* (De 28695)

EDDIE DEAN *I Dreamed of a Hillbilly Heaven* (Sage & Sand 180)
[several versions of this song were also recorded by Tex Ritter; all mention Jimmie Rodgers]

HAWKING BROTHERS *Will Hank Williams Meet Jimmie Rodgers?* (RZ G25421)

WILLIE PHELPS *Hank Williams Meets Jimmie Rodgers/So Long Pal Jimmie* (Driftwood EP1)

ED NICHOLLS *Jailhouse Yodel/ There's Nothing in My Heart But the Blues* (MH Records)

RED RIVER DAVE *Railroad Station in the Sky* (Reveal RV92768)

HANK SNOW *Salutes Jimmie Rodgers* [LP] (Vi LPM3131); *Jimmie Rodgers' Songs* [LP] (LPM2043); *Jimmie Rodgers Story* [LP] (LSP4708)

BENNIE HESS & TOM SWATZELL *The Ballad of Jimmie Rodgers* (Showland 241973)

KEN SERRATT *Memories of Jimmie Rodgers* (?Capitol)

BUDDY WILLIAMS *Sings Jimmie Rodgers* [LP] (Columbia 330SX7665)

ELTON BRITT *Jimmie Rodgers Blues* (Camden CAL/CAS2295)

JIMMIE SKINNER *Sings Jimmie Rodgers* [LP] (Mercury MG20700)

JACK ELLIOTT *Sings Jimmie Rodgers and Woody Guthrie* [LP] (Columbia 33SX1291)

GRANDPA JONES *Yodelling Hits* [LP] (London HA-U8119)

YODELING SLIM CLARK *Sings the Legendary Jimmie Rodgers Songs* [LP] (Palomino 300)

EDDIE NOACK *Remembering Jimmie Rodgers* [LP] (Wide World WWS2001)

MERLE HAGGARD *Same Train – Different Time* [LP] (Capitol SWBB223)

VARIOUS ARTISTS *When Evening Shadows Fall* [LP] (Vi LSP4073)

VARIOUS ARTISTS *Gone But Not Forgotten* [LP] [songs made famous by Jimmie Rodgers and others] (Marble Arch MAL1128)

Notes

1 / Rough and Rowdy Ways

1. See Charters, *The Bluesmen* (Oak Publications, 1967) and Oliver, *The Story of the Blues* (Barrie & Rockliff/Cresset Press, 1969).
2. Letter from Jake Smith to the authors (2 November 1972).
3. Mrs Jimmie Rodgers, *My Husband Jimmie Rodgers* (*Jimmie Rodgers' Life Story*) (Ernest Tubb Publications, 1953) 3.
4. Jerry Silverman, *The Folk Blues* (Macmillan, 1958) 9.
5. ibid.
6. Alan Lomax, *Folksongs of North America* (Doubleday & Co., 1960) 67.
7. Rodgers 7.
8. Nolan Porterfield, *Stranger Through Your Town* (unpublished monograph) 9.
9. ibid. 7.
10. Rodgers 56-7.
11. Claudia Rigby-Vick, quoted in Bill Malone, *Country Music, U.S.A.* (University of Texas Press, 1968) 85.
12. Rodgers 17.
13. ibid. 24.

2 / A Brakeman's Blues

1. Rodgers 218.
2. ibid. 27.
3. Letter in the possession of Anita Rodgers Court.
4. Rodgers 57.

5.   Billy Terrell, 'Billy Terrell's Comedians', *Blue Yodeler* 2:2 (Spring 1954) 3.
6.   ibid.
7.   ibid.
8.   Quoted in Malone 85.
9.   Malone 19.
10. Cliff Carlisle, interviewed by Eugene Earle, Lexington, Kentucky, 1957.
11. Letter from Nolan Porterfield to the authors, 11 July 1973.
12. Included on the Hank Snow LP *The Jimmie Rodgers Story* (RCA LSA-3107).
13. Rodgers 45-6.
14. Letter from Nolan Porterfield to the authors, 6 October 1973.
15. Quoted in Charles K. Wolfe, 'The Tennessee Ramblers – Ramblin' On', *Old Time Music* 13 (Summer 1974) 6-7.
16. Rodgers 70.
17. Dave Samuelson, notes to *The Tenneva Ramblers* (Puritan 3001).
18. Rodgers 67.
19. Quoted in Robert Shelton and Burt Goldblatt, *The Country Music Story* (Bobbs-Merrill, 1966) 151.
20. David Evans, 'Black Musicians Remember Jimmie Rodgers', *Old Time Music* 7 (Winter 1972/3) 13.
21. Rodgers 92.
22. Evans 14.
23. Rodgers 211.

3 / No Hard Times

1.   Ralph Peer, 'Jimmie Rodgers', Meridian *Star*, 26 May 1953, 24.
2.   Archie Green, 'Hillbilly Music: Source and Symbol', *Journal of American Folklore* 78:309 (July-September 1965) 204-28.
3.   Peer 24.
4.   ibid.
5.   Quoted in Malone 86.
6.   Cf. Charles K. Wolfe, 'Ralph Peer At Work: The Victor 1927 Bristol Sessions', *Old Time Music* 5 (Summer 1972) 12.
7.   Peer 24.
8.   ibid.
9.   Quoted in Wolfe, 'Ralph Peer At Work', 12.
10. ibid.
11. Peer 24.
12. Quoted in John Atkins (ed.), *The Carter Family* (Old Time Music Publications, 1973) 6.
13. Rodgers 98.
14. ibid. 100.
15. ibid. 109.
16. Peer 24.
17. ibid.
18. ibid.

19. ibid.
20. Rodgers 121.
21. Letter from Brian Rust to the authors, 17 November 1973.
22. Peer 24.
23. Rodgers 146-7.
24. Tony Russell, 'Kelly Harrell And The Virginia Ramblers', *Old Time Music* 2 (Autumn 1971) 8.
25. Rodgers 152.
26. ibid. 156.

4 / *Jimmie the Kid*

1. Elsie McWilliams, 'Jimmie Rodgers' Assistant', *Blue Yodeler* 1:4 (Fall 1953) 1.
2. Peer 24.
3. Wolfe, 'Ralph Peer At Work', 14.
4. Peer 24.
5. John Atkins, letter to the authors, 7 May 1973.
6. Rodgers 185.
7. McWilliams 1.
8. Rodgers 159.
9. ibid.
10. McWilliams 1.
11. ibid.
12. Rodgers 158.
13. ibid. 165.
14. ibid. 177.
15. ibid. 180.
16. ibid.
17. Reprinted in *Country And Western Express* 28 (February 1972) 7.
18. ibid.
19. ibid.
20. Rodgers 168.
21. ibid. 181.
22. Regal-Zonophone supplement RZ 27, March 1935.
23. Rodgers 187.
24. Peer 24.
25. Bristol *Herald-Courier,* 28 October 1928, quoted in Wolfe, 'The Discovery of Jimmie Rodgers: a Further Note', *Old Time Music* 9 (Summer 1973) 24.
26. Rodgers 194.
27. Malone 89.
28. Bill Bruner, interviewed in the *Dixie Times Picayune,* 24 May 1953, 7-8.
29. ibid. 8.
30. Malone 93.
31. Rodgers 211.
32. Sydonia M. Young, 'Jimmie Rodgers', *Pictorial History of Country Music Vol. 4* (Heather Publications, 1970) 34.

33. Publicity material reproduced in Shelton & Goldblatt 68.
34. Rodgers 232.
35. Russell, art. cit. (Ch. 3, note 24) 8.

5 / The T.B. Blues

1. Porterfield 7.
2. Interviewed by Oscar Huff and Jimmy Ramsey, Georgia, 1959.
3. ibid.
4. Interviewed by Fred Hoeptner and Bob Pinson, Lexington, Kentucky, 1959.
5. Rodgers 228.
6. Malone 89.
7. ibid.
8. Reproduced in *Pictorial History of Country Music Vol. 4* (Heather Publications, 1970) 33.
9. Quoted in the *Meridian Memorial Day Program* (1953) 6.
10. Tony Russell, 'The Freeny Story', *Old Time Music* 8 (Spring 1973) 15-19.
11. ibid.
12. Rodgers 238-9.
13. ibid. 240.
14. ibid. 241.
15. ibid. 237.
16. ibid. 234.
17. Porterfield 4.
18. ibid.
19. Interview with Earle (cf. Ch. 2, note 10).
20. Quoted in Atkins (ed.), *The Carter Family,* 7.
21. ibid. 9.

6 / The Last Blue Yodel

1. Malone 90.
2. Rodgers 227.
3. ibid. 227-8.
4. Letter from Jimmie Rodgers to Clayton McMichen, reproduced in Shelton & Goldblatt 65.
5. Letter from Clayton McMichen to the authors, 6 February 1969.
6. Rodgers 247.
7. ibid.
8. ibid. 246.
9. Terrell 4.
10. ibid.
11. Rodgers 252.
12. Letter from Dwight Butcher to the authors, 12 January 1971.
13. Malone 91.
14. Rodgers 259.
15. ibid. 261.

7 / *Jimmie Rodgers in Retrospect*

1. Letter from Dwight Butcher to the authors, 11 January 1969.
2. See, for example, Riley Crabtree's *When Hank Williams Met Jimmie Rodgers* (Columbia 21218) or The Virginia Rounders' *Hank Williams Meets Jimmie Rodgers* (Rosemay 1).
3. Peer 24.
4. Letter from Nolan Porterfield to the authors, 11 July 1973.
5. Rodgers 188.
6. Roy Horton, liner notes to *Country Music Hall of Fame (RCA* LPM-2531).
7. Malone 92.
8. Kenneth Allsop, *Hard Travellin'* (Hodder & Stoughton, 1967) 11-15.
9. Victor catalogue, c. 1931.
10. John Greenway, 'Folksong Discography', *Western Folklore* XXI: 1 (January 1960) 71.
11. Paul Oliver, 'Jimmy Rodgers', *Recorded Folk Music* 2:[2] (March-April 1959) 10.
12. Porterfield 1.
13. Ernest Tubb & Hank Snow, 'Remembering Jimmie Rodgers', *Billboard,* 16 May 1953, 20.
14. Malone 91-2.
15. Quoted in Malone 92.
16. Greenway 71.
17. Tex Ritter, interviewed by the authors, London, March 1970.
18. Patsy Montana, interviewed by the authors, London, June 1972.
19. Tony Russell, 'Kelly Harrell and the Virginia Ramblers', 8.
20. Malone 100.
21. Letter from John Edwards to George Tye, 23 December 1953.
22. 'Jesse Rogers', *Country Song Roundup* 1:8 (October 1950) 5.
23. Letter from Nolan Porterfield to the authors, 6 October 1973.
24. ibid.
25. Letter from Prynce Wheeler to the authors, 14 July 1973.
26. Carrie Rodgers in *Jimmie Rodgers Fan Club Newsletter* [undated].
27. *Billboard* LXXIII: 42, 30 October 1961, 68.
28. Quoted in Alice Foster, 'I Take A Lot Of Pride In What I Am', *Sing Out!* 19:5 (March 1970) 16.
29. Jack Elliott, *The Songs of Woody Guthrie and Jimmie Rodgers* (Columbia 33SX1291).
30. Evans 12.
31. Quoted in Stephen Calt & Rob Fleder, 'Nobody Had To Ask Me To Play the Blues', *Sing Out!* 21:1 (January 1971) 14.
32. Porterfield 14-15.
33. Paul Oliver, *Screening The Blues* (Cassell & Co, 1968).
34. Allsop 274.
35. John Greenway, 'Jimmie Rodgers — A Folksong Catalyst', *Journal of American Folklore* LXX:277 (July-September 1957) 232.
36. Malone 94.

8 / The Jimmie Rodgers Discography

1. Vi 21433 was originally released entitled *If Brother Jack Were Here*, with the composer credit to Jimmie Rodgers. Edward B. Marks and Joseph W. Stern, who actually composed the song years earlier, sued for credit and royalties. The original issue was quickly withdrawn and all subsequent issues bore the title and composer credits shown in the Discography.

2. E.T. Cozzens plays steel guitar on the first and last instrumental breaks, and mandolin on the middle two breaks. Rodgers could play mandolin but it is unlikely to be his playing on this record. Some issues of *Dear Old Sunny South by the Sea* and *The Sailor's Plea* are labelled as by Jimmie Rodgers and The Three Southerners. For matrices 41736, 41737 and 41739 Victor files list accompaniments as by The Three Southerners only, with no more detailed account of the instrumentation on each title; the details given in the Discography are our own speculation.

3. Although *Treasure Untold* was the form in which this piece was copyrighted, all issues were as *Treasures Untold*.

4. Vi A1454 shows B-6225-B and take-1 in the wax. In fact matrix 45099-1 appears on Bb B-6225-B, and the Vi A1454 pressing of *Blue Yodel No. 2* is identical to all other issues.

5. Vi 21574 and the LP reissues give the correct title as shown, but all other 78 rpm issues erroneously give it as *My Little Old Home Town in New Orleans*.

6. The R suffix to the take-number indicates a dubbing, usually, if not always, from the take preceding the one shown. The files do not indicate when this was done.

7. The Canadian issue of Vi 22523 is labelled *High Powered Mama, Get Yourself in Gear*.

8. The Burke Brothers have been referred to as the Burks Brothers by several writers. We have used the spelling Burke throughout, following the example of the Victor files.

9. Some issues have the composer credit (Arr. Rodgers).

10. The title is given as *The Gambler's Blues* on RZ MR911.

11. The Canadian issue of Vi 22523 is labelled *Jail House No. 2*.

12. This personnel, long considered merely hypothetical, has been confirmed by a Victor session sheet reported by Nolan Porterfield.

13. Victor files give *The Carter Family Interview Jimmie Rodgers* as an alternative title for this recording. Note that the title was changed again for the final take (69428-4, for which see below).

14. Two takes of 69428 are included on RA5645 but are identical. It is presumed that they are supposed to be takes -3 and -4.

15. The LP versions of this title differ slightly from all extant 78 rpm versions. Near the end of the recording Rodger's repetition of the

words 'town tonight' has been edited out, and his final speaking part ('Well, well, so I finally got up here to see you Carter Family . . .') has been dubbed in from take -3. The reason for this is not clear.

16. The title is given on RZ MR2795 as *Round Up Time Out West (When the Cactus is in Bloom)*.

17. This recording was originally titled *My Dog-Faced Gal*, and a rejected take exists with this title, but all issues were labelled *What's It?*

18. Tw FT1925 credits the Louisville Jug Band on the label.

19. It may be assumed that this is the same man as the Fred Koons on the previous days' recordings.

20. These issues are labelled *Blue Yodel* only.

21. The A suffix indicates Machine A, which recorded simultaneously with the machine that took down the unsuffixed takes. Thus -1 is identical to -1A and so forth. We have distinguished them in the Discography purely to show which take actually appears on the issued pressings.

22. Apparently this master was accidentally destroyed.

23. Some issues give a composer credit to Billy (or B.) Hill.

24. Victor files do not specify the accompaniment; however, on the aural evidence of *Mississippi Delta Blues,* where Colicchio is known to be playing guitar, the difference in style and timbre seems to indicate the line-up we have given.

25. All issues are labelled *Years Ago* except RZ MR1702, which is titled as shown.

26. Rodgers's long guitar solo after the fourth verse is edited out of this dubbed version.

Bibliography

Books

ALLEN, Frederick Lewis. *Only Yesterday*. Harper and Brothers, New York, 1931.
ATKINS, John [ed.] *The Carter Family*. Old Time Music, London, 1973.
ALLSOP, Kenneth. *Hard Travellin'*. Hodder and Stoughton, London, 1967.
CHARTERS, Sam. *The Country Blues*. Michael Joseph, London, 1960.
CHARTERS, Sam. *The Bluesmen*. Oak Publications, New York, 1967.
EVANS, David. *Tommy Johnson*. Studio Vista, London, 1971.
FERRIS, William, Jr. *Blues From the Delta*. Studio Vista, London, 1970.
GENTRY, Linnell. *History and Encyclopedia of Country And Western And Gospel Music*. McQuiddy Press, Nashville, 1961.
GODRICH, John, and DIXON, Robert M. W. *Blues & Gospel Records 1902 – 1942*. Storyville Publications, London, 1969.
LOMAX, John. *Folksongs of North America*. Doubleday, New York, 1960.
MALONE, Bill C. *Country Music U.S.A*. University of Texas Press, Austin, 1968.
MOORE, Thurston. *Pictorial History of Country Music* [four volumes]. Heather Publications, Denver, 1969–1972.
OLIVER, Paul. *Blues Fell This Morning*. Cassell, London, 1960.
OLIVER, Paul. *Screening the Blues*. Cassell, London, 1968.
OLIVER, Paul. *The Story Of The Blues*. Barrie & Rockcliff, The Cresset Press, London, 1969.
PORTERFIELD, Nolan. *Stranger Through Your Town*. [Unpublished monograph.]
RODGERS, Mrs. Jimmie. *Jimmie Rodgers' Life Story*. Ernest Tubb Publications, Nashville, 1953.
RUSSELL, Tony. *Blacks, Whites and Blues*. Studio Vista, London, 1970.
RUST, Brian. *The Victor Master Book: Volume 2 (1925-1936)*. Published by the author, Hatch End, 1969.
SHELTON, Robert and GOLDBLATT, Burt. *The Country Music Story*. Bobbs-Merrill, New York, 1966.
SILVERMAN, Jerry. *The Folk Blues*. Macmillan, London, 1958.

SPAETH, Sigmund. *A History of Popular Music in America*. Random House, New York, 1948.

Articles

CASE, Floy. 'Folk Music's First Lady – Mrs. Jimmie Rodgers'. *Cowboy Songs* (June 1955).

COMBER, Chris. 'The Singing Brakeman (film)'. *Opry* 1:6 (December 1968).

COMBER, Chris. 'Jesse Rogers'. *Country Music People* 1:10 (November 1970).

COMBER, Chris. 'Big Daddy Rodgers'. *Country Music Review* 1:9-11 (November 1972–January 1973).

DAVIS, Stephen F. 'The Country Music Heritage of Bristol, Tenn. -Va'. *Old Time Music 6* (Autumn 1972).

EDWARDS, John. 'America's Blue Yodeler'. *Discophile* 2 (Fall 1955).

EDWARDS, John. 'Memories of Jimmie Rodgers'. *Disc Collector 15* (c.1959).

EVANS, David. 'Black Musicians Remember Jimmie Rodgers'. *Old Time Music* 7 (Winter 1972/3).

GREEN, Archie. 'Hillbilly Music: Source and Symbol'. *Journal of American Folklore* 78:309 (July-September 1965).

GREENWAY, John. 'Jimmie Rodgers – A Folksong Catalyst'. *Journal of American Folklore* 70:277 (July-September 1957).

GREENWAY, John. 'Folksong Discography'. *Western Folklore* 21:1 (January 1960).

HAGGARD, Merle. 'I Take a Lot of Pride In What I Am'. *Sing Out!* 19:5 (April 1970).

HORTON, Roy. [Liner notes to *Country Music Hall of Fame* (RCA-Victor LPM 2531).]

LEE, Ian. 'Meridian Bound'. *Hillbilly Folk Record Journal* 1:4 (October 1954).

MANNING, Ed. 'The Story Of Jimmie Rodgers'. *Folkvoice* 12 (February 1964).

McELREA. Rodney. 'Jimmie Rodgers – The Caruso Of Country Music'. *Country News and Views* 4 (April 1966).

McWILLIAMS, Elsie. 'Jimmie Rodgers' Assistant'. *Blue Yodeler* 1:4 (Fall 1953).

McWILLIAMS, Elsie. 'Jimmie Rodgers'. Meridian *Star* (26 May 1953).

OLIVER, Paul. 'Jimmy Rodgers'. *Recorded Folk Music* 2: [3] (May/June 1959).

PEER, Ralph. 'Discovery of the First Hillbilly Great'. *Billboard* 65:200 (16 May 1953).

PEER, Ralph. 'Jimmie Rodgers'. Meridian *Star* (26 May 1953).

PEER, Ralph. Rodgers Heritage'. *Billboard* 66:21 (22 May 1954).

RODGERS, Carrie. 'Throw Your Things Together Kid'. *Billboard* 65:200 (16 May 1953).

RUSSELL, Tony. 'Kelly Harrell and the Virginia Ramblers'. Old Time Music 2 (Autumn 1971).

RUSSELL, Tony. 'A Pound Of Butter. Half A Dozen Eggs, And the Latest Jimmie Rodgers'. *Cream* 23 (April 1973).

RUSSELL, Tony. 'The Freeny Story'. *Old Time Music* 8 (Spring 1973).

STEWART-BAXTER, Derrick. 'The Story of Jimmie Rodgers'. *Jazz Journal* 6:5-6 (May-June 1953).

SAMUELSON, Dave. 'The Tenneva Ramblers'. [Liner notes to Puritan LP3001.] (March 1972).

TERRELL, Billy. 'Billy Terrell's Comedians'. *Blue Yodeler* 2:2 (Spring 1954).

TUBB, Ernest, and SNOW Hank. 'Rodgers Influence On Country Music'. *Billboard* 65:200 (16 May 1953).

TYE George. Jimmie Rodgers'. *Hillbilly Folk Record Journal* 1:1 (October 1954).

TYE, George. 'Jimmie Rodgers'. *Folkvoice* 2 (February 1959).

WILLIAMS, Bill [interviewed by Stephen Calt and Rob Fleder]. 'Nobody Had to Ask Me to Play the Blues'. *Sing Out!* 21:1 (January 1971).

WOLFE, Charles K. 'Ralph Peer At Work: The Victor 1927 Bristol Sessions'. *Old Time Music* 5 (Summer 1972).

WOLFE, Charles K. 'The Discovery Of Jimmie Rodgers: A Further Note'. *Old Time Music* 9 (Summer 1973).

WOLFE, Charles K. 'The Tennessee Ramblers: Ramblin' On'. *Old Time Music* 13 (Summer 1974).

YOUNG, Sydonia M. 'Jimmie Rodgers—America's Blue Yodeler'. *Pictorial History Of Country Music* Volume 4 (1972).

Uncredited articles

'Memorial To The Blue Yodeler'. *RCA-Victor Picture Record Review* 4:9 (May 1953)

'Blue Yodeler's Life Plagued By Illness'. *Billboard* 65:200 (16 May 1953).

'Jimmie Rodgers Story'. *Country Song Roundup* 1:25 (August 1953).

'Brakeman Who Turned His Voice Into Cash'. *Times-Picayune, Dixie Roto Magazine* 24 (May 1953).

'Tribute To Jimmie Rodgers'. *Country Song Roundup* 1:26 (October 1953).

'Rodgers Remembered'. *Newsweek* 41:23 (8 June 1953).

'Jesse Rogers'. *Country Song Roundup* 1:8 (October 1950).

'Bull Market In Corn'. *Time* 42:14 (October 1943).

Interviews

Cliff Carlisle, interviewed by Eugene Earle, Kentucky, 1957.
Cliff Carlisle, interviewed by Bob Powel, Kentucky, 1971.
Clayton McMichen, interviewed by Bob Pinson, Tennessee, 1957.
Patsy Montana, interviewed by the authors, London, 1972.
Tex Ritter, interviewed by the authors, London, 1970.
Gid Tanner, interviewed by Oscar Huff and Jimmie Ramsey, Georgia, 1959.

Unpublished letters

John Atkins to authors, 7 May 1973.
Dwight Butcher to authors, 11 January 1969; 12 January 1971.
John Edwards to George Tye, 23 December 1953.
Clayton McMichen to authors, 6 February 1969.
Nolan Porterfield to authors, 11 July 1973; 6 October 1973.
Mrs. Jimmie Rodgers to George Tye, 24 October 1953.
Brian Rust to authors, 17 November 1973.
Jake Smith to authors, 2 November 1972.
Prynce Wheeler to authors, 14 July 1973.

Index